Women of our Century

Leonie Caldecott

Leonie Caldecott was born in London in 1956 and educated at the French Lycée and Oxford. Since 1979 she
has worked as a freelance writer, and has been published in the *Guardian*, the *Sunday Times, Good House-
keeping, New Society* and other magazines. In 1982 she
was the winner of the Catherine Pakenham Memorial
Award for young women journalists. She has also contributed to several anthologies, including *Keeping the
Peace* (1983) and *Walking on the Water* (1983), and was co-
editor of a collection of women's writing on the environment, *Reclaim the Earth*, also published in 1983. She is
currently working on a book about women and Christianity.

LEONIE CALDECOTT

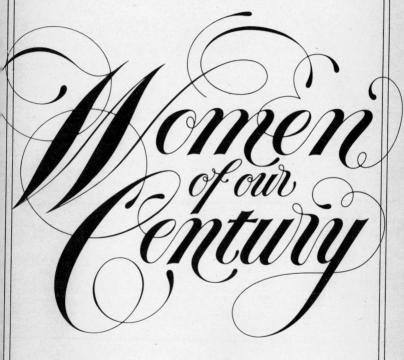

Women of our Century

ARIEL BOOKS

BRITISH BROADCASTING CORPORATION

For Pamela,
for Roseline, for Moyra,
for Jill and for Daphne,
with love.

The television series *Women of our Century* was first shown on
BBC 2 in 1984. The interviewers were Leonie Caldecott, Ann
Clwyd, Germaine Greer, Joanna Lumley, Bel Mooney and Polly
Toynbee. Louise Panton was Producer, Jill Dawson Assistant
Producer and Angela Jacobs Production Assistant.

Paule Vézelay died on 20 March 1984, after the book went to
press.

Picture credits

BBC HULTON PICTURE LIBRARY 3 (photo, Malcolm Dunbar), 15; CAMERA PRESS 5
(photo, John Goldblatt); KEYSTONE PRESS AGENCY 19; NAOMI MITCHISON 2, 4;
PRESS ASSOCIATION 24; PRINCIPAL & FELLOWS OF SOMERVILLE COLLEGE, OXFORD
21; DAME FLORA ROBSON 16; DORA RUSSELL 11, 12, 13; DAME JANET VAUGHAN 18, 20;
PAULE VÉZELAY 7, 8, 9; BARONESS WOOTTON OF ABINGER 23.
    The following photographs were specially taken by the BBC: 1, 6, 10, 14, 17, 22.

First published 1984

Published by the British Broadcasting Corporation,
35 Marylebone High Street, London W1M 4AA

Typeset by Phoenix Photosetting, Chatham
Printed in England by Mackays of Chatham Ltd

ISBN 0 563 20271 8

Contents

Acknowledgements

One is never so aware of being indebted to others as when one works under pressure of time, and a host of people helped me through the writing of this book in different ways. To begin with, I am indebted to those writers who first turned my attention to the task of reclaiming women's history and learning from it without fear of declaring one's personal interest; of these Dale Spender in particular comes to mind. In the case of this book, I am indebted to the research, enthusiasm and encouragement of Celia Lowenstein. Each of the women I wrote about generously gave precious time and energy, and in all cases except that of Paule Vézelay and Dame Flora Robson, allowed me to quote extensively from their autobiographies (which, where published, are listed at the beginning of each chapter). Whilst writing about Flora Robson, I was greatly assisted by Kenneth Barrow's excellent biography published in 1981. In the case of Paule Vézelay, I gained some useful insights through the researches of Sarah Wilson of the Courtauld Institute. I am also indebted to the five other women who interviewed my subjects for the BBC television series that this book is designed to accompany, and who gave permission for me to use that material, as well as to the producer of the series, Louise Panton, who initiated me with great good humour into a new medium. Still at the BBC, thanks are due to Jill Dawson, and most especially to Angela Jacobs, who was a tower of strength and patience as I invaded the office or telephoned in a desperate search for books and other background material. I am grateful to Deborah Rogers for her unfailing faith in me, to Philippa Brewster for giving me a sabbatical from a long-standing commitment so that I could take up this project, and most of all to Sheila Elkin of the BBC, who maintained a remarkable sang-froid in the face of my inability to meet tight schedules, and whose interest and belief in the book kept me going through the darkest moments. Finally, I should also like to thank Susan Griffin and Stratford Caldecott, each of whom saw me through different stages of this book and gave me invaluable support at every level.

Introduction

When I started work on this book, it was with mixed feelings of curiosity and slight trepidation. On the one hand, I was keen to learn about a period of history immediately preceding my own era, to hear first-hand accounts of events, many of which have a bearing on my own life; and in particular, to hear these accounts from members of my own sex. Many women of my generation are turning to the lives of women who came before us in order to understand factors underlying our own experience, and I am no exception. On the other hand, the history of the century into whose latter half I was born is not something on which I was always entirely clear. How exactly had the vote, two world wars, social and economic upheavals, changes (both positive and negative) in the role and image of women, affected myself and other members of my sex? It was as though, the closer events were to the start of my own life, the less clearly I could focus on them, rather like someone long-sighted trying to read a book at arm's length, and finding their arm just isn't long enough.

There are many ways in which one can try to grasp historical material. Personally, I have never been on terribly friendly terms with dates and statistics, far less with the power-play of nations and the composition of human institutions. I rarely feel I have understood something unless I have in some way literally *stood under* it: that's to say put myself on the inside of it, imaginatively or emotionally. So the experience of talking, informally and personally, to six women roughly the age of this century about the shape and meaning of their lives, has been a good way of coming to know that century a little better.

Not that this activity has left me with a comprehensive knowledge of previously hazy areas. For one thing, the six women whose portraits I have sketched here are by no means representative, when you take twentieth-century British society as a whole. They all come from comfortable, middle-class backgrounds. They all received a relatively good education, this in the early years of the century being private rather than state-provided, and in some cases being due more to parental enthusiasm and encouragement than to the intrinsic merits of their schools or governesses. And they all went on to make a mark in their chosen fields, to make the most of opportunities which opened up for them, each living her life to the full, a characteristic which was brought home to me by the fact that each of them was still utterly absorbed in her work when I met her.

These are the immediate descendants of the Victorian feminists, who campaigned for women's rights and suffrage in the face of considerable scorn and derision. Born at the turn of the century, in the decade of what *Punch* magazine tried to deride as the 'New Woman', they grew up amidst the apparent security of the Edwardian era, coming of age with its collapse during the First World War. Their mothers got the long-awaited vote that they, in their supposedly irresponsible twenties, did not, and those of them who went to Oxford or Cambridge could not yet receive the degrees their male contemporaries were awarded after sitting the same exams. In middle age they lived through yet another World War, followed by a decade devoted to economic recovery through vastly increased industrialisation, the era of the angry young men and (a curious counterpart) the saccharine promise of the 'feminine mystique'. They reached retirement age during the exhibitionistic idealism of the sixties, and as they entered their seventh and eighth decades, the world slid into recession, dogged by increasing violence amongst individuals and nations, not to mention a newly spiralling arms race. Against the background of uncertainty, however, the women's movement has once again manifested itself to a degree not seen since the beginning of the century.

Not every woman in this book would agree with my view that within the stirrings and various expressions of the women's movement lies the most interesting perspective on social and psychological changes brought about during the last eighty-four years or so. Only two of them describe themselves unreservedly as feminists. And yet, I feel, it is because they are women that they have something to teach us: for instance about survival in the face of social pressures which, in their youth, were not entirely conducive to female independence of body and mind. They have each, in one way or another, coped with loss and discouragement in both their private and their professional lives. Yet these are all strong, courageous women who knew what they wanted and worked to achieve it. Whether they married or remained single, none of them subsided into passive dependence on a man. The ones who bore children combined this role with the work in which they were already immersed. Doubtless their social and economic backgrounds contributed to this strength. But that doesn't diminish the fact that the rest of us can be grateful for their example and inspiration. In this sense, as well as in the more obvious political sense, I echo Barbara Wootton when she writes: 'Others broke open the doors and I walked through.'

The lessons which come out of these lives differ in each case; none of these women can be forced into a generalised mould. I have tried to take each one very much on her own terms. Where I have intervened with my own comments, it is because I felt (as in the case of Dora Russell) that the more unusual elements in their lives needed some clarification. Obviously I have been hampered in this by my own presuppositions and prejudices, and in that respect, these portraits are highly personal. They are my tribute to six interesting and stimulating women, women who have reminded me once again that, as Naomi Mitchison says, 'to be a woman is a rather splendid thing'.

Naomi Mitchison

Naomi Mitchison, born 1897 as Naomi Haldane, married G. R. Mitchison in 1916. Her first book, published in 1923, was an historical novel called *The Conquered*. This was the first of over eighty books on many varied subjects that she has written. Her work has ranged from novels, short stories and poetry to writing on contemporary political and social subjects and books for children. Her autobiography begins in *Small Talk* (1973) and continues in *All Change Here* (1975) and *You May Well Ask* (1979). An early novel, *The Corn King and the Spring Queen* (1931), has recently been reissued by Virago who are planning to follow this with other reprints. Naomi Mitchison was interviewed for the television series by Leonie Caldecott.

'I hate habits, however "good", and I hate making a pattern out of life. Life is destroyed that way.' (1930)

'I'm one of those old women who sit in the corner by the fire, and people come and sit on the ground in front of her and say, tell me another.' (1983)

Naomi Mitchison

The most vivid image I have of Naomi Mitchison comes from watching her walking around the large and multifarious garden at Carradale in Scotland, her home base for nearly fifty years. She was naming the plants for me. There were an incredible variety of rhododendrons. Down at the bottom of the garden, over a wind-blown field, was the sea.

Having talked to Naomi Mitchison about her life, Carradale seemed to me at once a haven and a stepping-off point. The woman by my side was thoroughly rooted here. Yet, I felt, this very rootedness gave her the freedom to set out on innumerable journeys. I could visualise her walking out of her front door and down to the sea, stepping casually into a small waiting boat and disappearing over the water.

Everything about Naomi Mitchison bespeaks a kind of fearlessness. Her movements are decisive and energetic. Her face, whose strong features and uncompromising expressions were once captured in the drawings of Wyndham Lewis, has lost none of its intensity. It has, naturally enough, gained a great many lines, which, when she reflects on some question you have asked her, almost swallow up the rest of the face in a movement of concentration, a sort of indrawing out of which her eyes will suddenly emerge to fix yours with their piercing blue gaze. Those eyes are what I see when I think of her frank and witty responses to my often rather intimate questions about her life.

Watching Naomi Mitchison go about her business inside her large and rambling house, entertaining an endless stream of family and other visitors, then striding through her garden to feed the pig, there is precious little point in trying to persuade her to expend a little less energy. She is unstoppable. As we talked (she was tired of talking about herself and wanted to hear about me instead), she kept bending down to do a little weeding, or to pick a lettuce and some radishes for dinner.

Then she interrupted our conversation and dived into a

particularly thick patch of foliage by the side of the house. Out came the secateurs, and a purposeful clipping began. There's a small rhododendron bush here, she said, a trifle breathlessly, being smothered by its neighbours. I hadn't seen the bush myself, but sure enough, after about ten minutes' work on her part, it emerged into daylight. (Several months later, I found the sight of women clipping away the perimeter fence at Greenham Common strangely reminiscent of this scene.)

This faintly ruthless protection of the small and weak against the more powerful and exuberant forces of nature is as much a part of Naomi Mitchison as her adventurous spirit. In all our conversations, she struck me as a woman who knew how to draw happiness from every aspect of her life: work, love, motherhood, travel, friendship, politics. Reviewing the third part of Naomi's autobiography, *You May Well Ask*, in 1979, her contemporary Dora Russell described this quality very well.

'Her life accords with her code; a life entirely concerned with creation, whether in mind, spirit, or ordinary practical affairs. To me this represents what (stripped of labels of class or degree of intelligence) is meant by being a woman.'

This rich and varied life began in Edinburgh on 1 November 1897. Naomi's father was the physiologist and philosopher John Scott Haldane, who did pioneering work on air and ventilation, work which took him from checking the safety of collieries to the design of gas masks in the First World War. Her mother was Louisa Kathleen Trotter, high Tory and passionate feminist all in one, a beautiful woman with strong views which were apt to conflict with the liberalism of the Haldanes (her brother-in-law Richard was Liberal Lord Chancellor).

Naomi describes her mother as having been 'very keen on the Empire and all that, but with a sense of duty towards other people, and a genuine compassion and feeling towards, for instance, the miners who came to the house because of my father's work. It was a kind of Toryism which I'm afraid is a little bit rare nowadays.'

Although the family came from Scotland, the majority of Naomi's childhood (which she describes in the first part of her auto-biography, *Small Talk*) was spent in Oxford, where her father pursued his research. It was a secure, stable upbringing, with all the trappings of the Edwardian era. 'You felt you knew what a boring life you were going to have,' remembers Naomi with a smile. 'Everything would always stay the same. How wrong we were!'

As children, she and her brother Jack (or 'Boy', as she called him) were very close. He was her senior by five years, and quickly followed in his father's footsteps, becoming a biologist and geneticist. The two children did mild experiments on one another, sniffing chloroform, 'but sensibly we did it standing up, and when we felt we were going to fall down, we stopped.' They also bred guinea-pigs, making Mendelian notes about the colouring and other characteristics of the succeeding generations. If any of the pregnant females died, Naomi had no hesitation in performing a post-mortem in order to find out the colours of the unknown litter.

Naomi describes herself as having a love-hate relationship with science. Her father had a laboratory in their house at Cherwell, and she was sometimes enlisted as lab assistant. She would be asked to watch her father conducting one of his breathing experiments on himself in a large metal chamber, with instructions to pull him out and perform artificial respiration, should he keel over unconscious.

'As it happened, he was always all right,' she says with her characteristic aplomb, 'but he knew he could trust me to do the right thing if anything did go wrong.'

She herself, however, did not become a scientist. She attributes this in part to her emotional involvement with her subjects. Her guinea-pigs, she says, were highly anthropomorphised. She once even squeezed milk from a female's teat in order to taste it. A more likely factor in her not becoming a scientist would be the somewhat truncated nature of her education. In earlier childhood, she attended the Dragon School in Oxford, where her brother Jack had been sent before progressing to Eton. This was a boys' school which took the occasional girl, until puberty exiled her, as it did in Naomi's case with the onset of menstruation at the age of twelve.

'I was for all practical purposes a boy until the awful thing happened,' she wrote in *Small Talk*. '. . . I had little or no pubic hair; my breasts were ungrown and did not in fact develop until my mid-teens. And then there was blood on my blue serge knickers. I was quickly pulled out of school and I never went back. I couldn't understand why, only it seemed that it was something about me which was shameful and must above all never be mentioned to a school friend. It had been a complete surprise, because I had not taken in my mother's carefully veiled and no doubt physiologically inaccurate information.'

After this, she was educated at home with a governess and

four other girls of her own age. She might have been sent to a public school like her brother, only 'a good deal of gentle pressure was put on me to stay at home, because after all my brother would soon be starting at New College, and we'd all be together.' The governess, in spite of being a benign presence in the household, was not able to provide the young Haldane intellect with all the meat it needed. In order to pass university entrance exams at sixteen, she needed extra coaching in Latin and Maths. Comparing her development with that of her brother, Naomi Mitchison was later to reflect on the impact of sex-roles in the education of her day, even for children whose parents were relatively enlightened.

'I grew out of childhood with a healthy respect for scientific curiosity and work, but I never had my brother's early understanding of it, and I wonder, now, whether this was temperamental or whether certain avenues of understanding were closed to me by what was considered suitable or unsuitable for a little girl. Not deliberately closed, I think, since both my parents believed in feminine emancipation, but – there is a difference between theory and practice.'

In some ways, she says, she was quite an ambitious little girl. She thought of becoming a doctor, something which was encouraged by her mother, who in the 1880s had herself entertained the thought of becoming a doctor, though had never been able to realise the ambition. Here the question of theory and practice becomes very important. Naomi's mother was a feminist in the sense that she believed women were equal, and given the opportunity, could do as well as their male counterparts. She thought women should have the vote. And yet she was opposed to the militant suffragettes, 'because she felt they were so unladylike, even unfeminine, and that you mustn't do things this way; you must always keep within the law.' There was a limit to how far she was prepared to go to change the position of her sex, and this included her daughter. Hers was a distinctly conservative feminism, which went hand in hand with a philanthropy based, as it were, on 'noblesse oblige' and 'being a lady'.

So in spite of encouraging her daughter and being pleased when she went to Oxford University as a home student, Kathleen Haldane's priorities were very much centred around the question of propriety. Naomi describes the experience of being a girl at the turn of the century and before the First World War as 'feeling one were in a cage all the time'. She wore woolly combinations which came below the knee. Most of her physical needs, from food to laundry, and even to having her hair brushed, were taken care of by servants. Everywhere she went, she was accompanied by a chaperon (this continued even after she was married and had her first child).

'Going to lectures, to a party, even going out for a couple of minutes on a London street, this good woman had to accompany me. It was as though one were surrounded by a den of lions!'

In the end, it was the life of the imagination that offered a way out of the cage. It also offered Naomi's interest in science another and ultimately broader outlet. Her childhood closeness to animals, her immersion in the natural life on the Cherwell river in Oxford and round her grandparents' home in Scotland, combined with the spirit of enquiry that surrounded her (not only within her family, but amongst friends such as the Huxleys), all fed a facility for recording nature in a somewhat different way from her kinsfolk.

'If I was anything, it was a good observer, not only of guinea-pigs and wild plants, but also of people, and especially of people in relation to myself, a not uncommon teenage interest.' The early writer of poems and plays, in which she and her friends performed, the little girl who had nightmares and canoed down the river telling herself stories, was busy developing her imagination, a faculty that would serve her far better, I suspect, than the microscope or the scalpel. She was destined to be an alchemist with words rather than a manipulator of cells or atomic particles.

Meanwhile her formal education continued to be on the science side. In 1914, she began reading science as a home student at what is now St Anne's College. But even this part of her education was cut short – by the onset of the First World War. She was sixteen, and like many people, was at first confident that the British would win and that it would 'all be over by Christmas'.

Then one of her brother's friends, Dick Mitchison, proposed to her. She knew Dick fairly well, having always found it easy to talk to him and even confide in him about the terror of her recurrent nightmares. But really, she thinks, she might well have become engaged to the first man in uniform ('I beg your pardon: the first *officer*') who had asked her. She had been feeling somewhat left out as her brother and his friends went off to collect their share of the glory.

At first, then, marriage seemed to her like a form of 'war work'. A way of being involved in the 'great excitement'. Yet reality soon came home to roost as hostilities did not end after a few months. The war settled into yet another routine – albeit a far grimmer, less pleasant routine – and there was no blaze of triumph, no end in sight, only the prospect of further months of anxiety and pain. 'Inexplicably we were not winning, and our friends began to get killed; really killed so that we would not see them again.' The adolescent girl whose mood had accorded with the First World War recruitment poster entitled *The Women of Britain Say Go* began slowly to face a more complex and cruel world than the one her mother had presented to her. The marriage, for its part, became a matter of 'racing against time'.

Before the knot was tied, Naomi persuaded her mother to let her go to St Thomas's Hospital in London and be a Voluntary Aid Detachment nurse. 'It was all very large, open wards, and there were no disposables as there are today, so anything like syringes had to be sterilised. A lot of the job consisted in cleaning up the toilets and that sort of thing. Some of the wounds I had to deal with were really horrifying, and seeing things like gas gangrene and people in great pain made a deep impression on me. In fact I fainted at my first bad dressing, but that was only because I had to look on and wasn't actually *doing* something. I think this is probably why my first novel, *The Conquered*, was so full of blood and gore – I was trying to exorcise it all.'

Naomi was also receiving letters from friends at the front. Her attitude to the war was changing. 'After the Gallipoli landings, one began to realise how many human lives were being sacrificed for very little military gain.' Rereading the letters now, and also those sent to her mother by older men, 'makes for a terrible embarrassment and sadness'. One letter written to her by an Old Etonian in 1915, after 'the dew of that early patriotism had dried away', ends on a chilling note.

'I had some extraordinarily unpleasant escapes, one shell exploding on my seat in the officers' mess about one minute before my occupation of it . . . I have a vast deal to say still on the subject of war but the flies make letter-writing impossible and as I shall indubitably be killed before returning to England you will probably never hear it; which is a pity as it will probably aggravate you intensely.'

She remembers, also, reading the first of Siegfried Sassoon's poems which was published in *The Times*. 'I thought, my goodness, this is it . . .'

Naomi and Dick were married in the Oxford registry office, in a fairly austere manner, while Dick was on short leave in 1916. The Mitchisons would have preferred a church wedding, but the

Haldanes, being 'highly moral agnostics' (Naomi's paternal grandmother told her that she must follow her conscience on the matter), were not worried. Soon afterwards, Dick was transferred out of his cavalry regiment to the Signals, swopping his horse for a motorbike. Then he had an accident, being thrown off the bike and having his skull fractured. As next of kin, Naomi was rushed out to France, along with her father-in-law, to be with the young husband who might never, it was thought at first, regain his normal mental faculties.

It was a trying experience for an eighteen-year-old, even one with the degree of self-possession that Naomi had. She did not get on terribly well with her father-in-law, who was a rather withdrawn, formal man. Dick was often delirious, not recognising her and even attacking her verbally. She was suddenly very isolated, without anyone close to turn to for warmth and support.

The Sister on the ward, however, seems to have recognised the need to anchor Naomi to some sort of active role in the midst of all this insecurity. Discovering that she had done some nursing, she promptly enlisted the young woman's skills to nurse her own husband. 'The doctor had said Dick was going to die, but the Sister said he's going to pull through and you're going to help him.'

Her diary of the time bears witness to the courage, generosity and patience of the women who serviced the war, nursing the wounded and the dying, often with minimal resources in the way of trained staff and medical supplies. Sister, for example, she describes as an optimist, 'charming and professional, but not unnecessarily professional'. These were women who, in a crisis, made the best use of whatever lay to hand. Including a young woman hardly out of school, about whom the Sister knew next to nothing, in the life of the hospital, was an act of generosity and sensitivity that professional women have not always displayed towards other members of their sex, even in circumstances that were considerably less stressful.

There is another incident in the diary that illustrates the special relationships that were being forged amongst women in the heart of the war. On one of her last evenings before Dick was transferred to a convalescent hospital and she returned to England, Naomi went out walking in the Forêt d'Eu with two VAD nurses. It was still not exactly usual for women to go out alone together, especially in a foreign country and in war-time. But the three young women had a wonderful time, treating themselves to a slap-up meal in a country restaurant and sharing their life stories with one another, as women have done since time immemorial, whenever they have been able to find the time and the space to do it – which in a hospital in France in 1917 cannot have been very often. In common with everyone involved in the war, the VADs were working long hours for little reward: twelve and a half hours a day, with three hours off and short meal-times, one day off every two months, and a week's leave every eighteen months.

Perhaps the global crisis all about them sharpened their own critical faculties. Anyhow, they discussed the dilemmas that women face, and 'deplored the badness of a girl's schooling and how hard it is for her to make her way to any really educated work'.

Back home, Naomi started taking an interest in politics, stirring up local interest in the League of Nations by dint of a barrage of correspondence in the *Oxford Times*. 'I did not think it sensible to sign my own name; everyone would know I was only a girl even if I was married. So I signed them "Mother of Seven", "Returned Serviceman" and so on.' A revealing choice of roles when it comes to the issue of who has the right to express an opinion about how the world should be run!

The 'controversy' soon drew in others, amongst them many Oxford literati like Gilbert Murray, and the Oxford branch of the League of Nations Society was formed. Until the time came for the birth of her first baby, Naomi was its secretary. Whilst Dick was at the front, she was living at home (where she had her first confinement) and thus still very much under her mother's wing. The practice of chaperoning had continued (she couldn't even go alone to the League of Nations meetings) and didn't in fact stop until the day when, taking the train to join Dick on leave in Italy, she gave the anonymous woman entrusted with her virtue the slip, by losing herself amongst the crowds in the third-class compartments.

'I was married, but I had scarcely begun to be free, and I was being somewhat conditioned into not wanting this. When I had a house of my own, I was told, I would have to engage (and dismiss) servants, order food, see that everything was just so. But somehow I did not at all like the idea of all that and the one person from whom I couldn't learn it was my mother – or, I suppose, my mother-in-law. Nor would I have accepted, say, a domestic science course if it had been suggested from above. How stupid can one be! And yet perhaps I was clinging on to some part of me that had to grow, but only on its own.'

Once the war was over, however, and she and Dick set up house in London at last, with Dick pursuing his career at the bar once more, Naomi had to come to terms with the complexities of running a household with servants, babies (for she soon had several more), work and social life. Of course the last three were made possible by the first. Looking back on her privileged upper-middle-class background, she neither disowns it nor shrouds it in a cloud of half-heartedly conservative nostalgia.

'We have to remember that what seems odd or even shocking today, was not so yesterday. We can't be sure which of the actions and habits and relationships of today will seem all wrong tomorrow; don't let's be too certain who to blame for what.'

It was certainly the domestic help that enabled her to start writing professionally. She believes that nowadays, a woman even in her social position has a much harder time of it. 'Household gadgets are not nearly as efficient as human beings, and of course domestic help was extraordinarily cheap. I later told Nurse, who came from the Highlands and was a good friend, that I felt terrible about having paid her so little. "But you're not remembering," she replied, "what a lot one could get for a pound note in those days."'

In any case, Naomi Mitchison would have written, though she might not have written so much. Wherever she found herself, she would scribble away – whilst pushing a pram in the park, or going round and round the Circle line on the underground (a good place, she says, to avoid the usual interruptions). In her early twenties, she was having many vivid dreams which she started turning into plays and short stories.

Then one day Dick read one of her plays, and mentioned that the setting reminded him of the sixth century AD. 'What was going on then? I had no idea, only knew I hated history.' Nonetheless, she was drawn into Gibbon – 'I was twenty-one, just the age for Gibbon' – and hence on to other historical writers. From that moment on she forgot her aversion to history as she had known it in school and devoured everything she could lay her hands on about ancient civilisations. She started writing historical fiction, which somehow enabled her to explore her contemporary concerns in a far more vivid and convincing context than her attempts at contemporary fiction had done.

'Before that I had started two or three modern novels, but as I was completely without direct experience of the emotional or social situations I had got into my plots, they were very bad and the main characters were all versions of myself, a common enough fault in young writers.'

In order to get her material, Naomi would not only read avidly, but also pick the brains of eminent historians such as Ernest Barker, H. T. Wade Gery and Maurice Bowra, or even Arnold Toynbee. The academics were often delighted to have their worlds cast into vivid detail by her pen.

The Conquered, which dealt with the conquest of Gaul by the Romans, was published in 1923 and was a great success. Naomi had broken with pre-war convention by using contemporary language in a historical novel. Thus she became part of a whole generation of novelists who blurred the rigid distinction between modern 'realism' and other-worldly 'fantasy'. She fed into her subject-matter all the experience, passions, and problems of a woman growing into the accelerating pace of the twentieth century. Amidst children, husband, friends, growing political concerns and creative work, Naomi Mitchison was beginning to stake an increasingly firm claim on her own life.

It was a happy time, though not without tragedy. In 1927, her eldest son Geoffrey caught meningitis and died. 'One recovers in a sense, but not completely,' she wrote later in *You May Well Ask*, a memoir of the years between the wars. 'One can look back beyond, but never without pain, never without some shadow of possible guilt. The sum of pain in the world has been increased by that fraction; it does not balance with anything.'

Motherhood seems in many ways to have been the greatest source of both pain and satisfaction to her. Almost all of her seven confinements (only five of her children have survived) were difficult, owing to a twisted pelvis resulting from an early childhood accident. Speaking of the children that died, and of the miscarriages in between, there is a deep sense of brooding. Looking at her thoughtful, puckered face, I sensed a great will to create life, and an almost organic retreat back into the darkest part of the self when that will is frustrated. She is not sentimental about her children, and certainly does not use them as a justi-fication for her own existence. But there is a formidable, a very womanly pride in having borne them and raised them.

She seems to have integrated her social life, her family life and her professional life rather well. She would feed a baby whilst reading novels to review for the feminist journal *Time and Tide*, for whom she specialised in French fiction, 'including I think the early Proust; of course one had no idea how long it was going to be, or I wouldn't have started . . .' She describes *Time and Tide* as the 'first avowedly feminist literary journal with any class, in many ways ahead of its time'. The editor, Lady Rhondda, was 'always tremendously encouraging and gave gorgeous parties. I remember driving back from one of them, cautiously since there had been a fair consumption of alcohol, but feeling splendid, as though the whole world was opening up and everything would work out, not only for myself, but for women in general.'

She was also on the editorial board of a journal called *The Realist*, aimed at bringing together the arts, the sciences and the humanities between the covers of one publication. She was the youngest member among an impressive list of names, chaired by Arnold Bennett.

A great many people, both well known and not so well known, frequented the Mitchisons' house, River Court, in Hammersmith. Childhood friends, such as the Huxleys and the Gielguds, also came. Naomi Mitchison and Lewis Gielgud sometimes collaborated over the writing of plays. 'We always thought we might manage one which his brother John or his friends would like!' But theatre was not to be a successful medium for her, though she had great fun visiting Gielgud in Paris to work on the plays.

'Lewis and I worked all evening until the exhaustion point, laughing like mad at our own jokes,' wrote Naomi in *You May Well Ask*. 'We would go to the local café or Chez Louise, where I occasionally danced with the lesbian professional ladies who came to eat and dance in congenial surroundings before they went to other bars to earn their living. Some had families to support. Louise herself was that way, with the barmaid as her wife. I remember once in the late thirties going there with Margaret Cole; Louise thought I had at last seen the light.'

The secret of Naomi Mitchison's ability to make friends and keep them must have had a great deal to do with her openness and her genuine curiosity about other people and how they saw the world. She often made friends through her reviewing of other writers' work – this is how she first got to know Stevie Smith, whose gift she recognised and tried to promote long before the literary establishment welcomed her into its bosom. Her description of Stevie Smith is a typical Mitchison thumbnail sketch.

'She looked like a bird, not an exotic bird but one of the plain-coloured English birds, restless hedge skirmishers, good survivors in any weather. But what she said was anything but bird-like; it was witty, full of meaning, one-off from a packed mind.'

Other friends of the time included E. M. Forster, who first wrote to her in 1923 to congratulate her on her novel *The Conquered*, W. H. Auden, Olaf Stapledon, H. G. Wells, Gerald Heard and Wyndham Lewis, who made many portraits of her. She would sit for him, and he would tease her by putting forward 'some impossible right-wing proposition' and then laughing when she refused to take the bait.

By this time she was beginning to take a serious interest in the world situation and politics in general, following historical novels like *Cloud Cuckoo land* and *The Corn King and the Spring Queen* with a contemporary novel largely set in the Soviet Union. This was *We Have Been Warned*, which after some problems with censorship (which led her to abandon her original publishers, Jonathan Cape) was published in 1936. Mitchison's writing had always been fairly sexually explicit, which had passed in the historical novels; but when the setting was contemporary Russia, this appeared to cause problems.

'There was a rape scene, done from a woman's point of view, and I don't think this had been done before. It's funny, because men's sexuality seems to have always been acceptable in the publishing world, yet they are, still now, I think, a bit fussy about women's.'

Naomi's interest in women's sexuality led to her involvement in the birth control campaign. She speaks with great warmth about Marie Stopes, whose book *Married Love* was the first genuine sex education book and which Naomi says transformed her marriage as well as many others. During the late twenties and thirties she helped run a birth control clinic in North Kensington. In 1929 she attended the World League for Sex Reform Congress, and delivered a paper which was published in 1930. Much of the paper is as relevant today as it was fifty years ago.

'When women have sufficient control over their external environment,' she wrote, looking to the future, 'to ensure that their work will be compatible with having babies, or when the whole business of having babies becomes a real job in itself, carrying with it social respect and economic independence – there are so many different possibilities – (contraception) will be still less necessary. One can vaguely see a position in which it will be least necessary of all, almost unnecessary, an anachronism belonging wholly to the Centuries of Industrial Complication, or whatever they choose to call us. This will be when women have sufficient control of their internal environment to ensure that their bodies will not suffer during pregnancy or parturition, and also perhaps, when their psycho-physical control becomes so complete that they can at their own will be fertile or not fertile.'

To some, that last sentence may sound fanciful, to some it may not. It has echoes of ideas recently voiced by radical feminists, and this makes Mitchison sound well ahead of her time. But these ideas are also perfectly consonant with her interest in anthropology, and the more mysterious components of ancient cultures and even contemporary non-Western cultures.

At any rate, Naomi Mitchison has always been open-minded about areas not deemed entirely acceptable by the scientific, political and economic theories left over from the nineteenth century. As a child, she knew Andrew Lang, who encouraged her to see fairies, though she always balanced her openness to that 'seeing through the gap' into another world, with a healthy scepticism (Lang once brought her in to give an opinion on the doctorate of a young man who was trying to prove the existence of fairies at Oxford – Naomi judged his evidence to be inadequate). In the early thirties, she was also interested in the theories of Gerald Heard, published in books like *The Emergence of Man* and *The Source of Civilisation*, which charted the alienation of modern man, with his extreme individualism, from what we might now (after Jung) call the collective unconscious.

She and a group of friends even experimented with the practical implications of some kind of 'group-mindedness', but eventually she let it drop and she returned to 'putting my faith into some kind of political or economic cure for our evils'. ('But,' she adds wryly, 'that didn't work either.')

Her views on marriage seem equally forward-looking. She and Dick Mitchison practised what might now be called an 'open marriage'. Each of them had lovers at various points of their lives, and their partner always knew about it. Yet their fundamental commitment was to the family unit and the children. I asked Naomi if there had been elements in this arrangement that are now ignored by couples touched by the sexual revolution of the sixties and the 'me' generation of the seventies. She replied that she did feel there was a tendency for younger generations to mistake sex for love (all her lovers, she says, were deeply loved) and to take sex for granted.

'Love is a difficult word, but I suppose it represents a kindness and a coming-together through people being, wanting to be, as good to one another as they can be.' Yet monogamy, she says, equals monotony.

'Love has a good many forms. There's the one where you're

certain of a permanent relationship of some kind, and that kind is perfectly compatible with having another kind of love relationship which will include sex with somebody else. It's a bad thing to be cornered in any way.' Though any deviation from old-fashioned monogamy, she says, should be seen against the background of a stable home in which there is a genuine respect and caring between husband and wife.

Between the Mitchisons there was a total trust. They each provided an indispensable emotional stability for the other, giving encouragement or a shoulder to cry on as it became necessary. This was the foundation on which the freedom of their relationship was built.

'You know the story of the man who marries the Fairy Swan Queen, and so long as he allows her to fly away when she needs to, she'll always come back, but if he seizes her and burns her wings, things turn bad? Well Dick would always let me go, and I'd do the same for him. And we always came back.'

Like some of her feminist contemporaries, Naomi looked forward to a time when women would be able to have children by different fathers if they chose to. Now, she feels that the situation has altered dramatically. 'The modern, serious and loving man is much more involved with his children than his counterpart of fifty years ago. I mean, after all, I go back to a time when husbands were never expected to know how to change a baby or bath a little wee one.'

It is perhaps in her views about sexuality that Naomi Mitchison emerges most vividly as a feminist. She comments wryly that whilst everyone was very shocked at mass sterilisation of men in India, not much gets said about enforced abortions in China.

Her involvement with politics did not end with the birth control campaign, however. Though she says she always knew that 'if I got really involved in politics, it would be exceedingly bad for my writing', she nonetheless felt the pull of early feminism, and a lingering disgust at the structures that had brought about the war, which led her towards a mild involvement with the Women's International League (though baby-broken nights, she says, kept her from giving it her entire attention).

Yet her mother's right-wing views, which had influenced her so much as a child (to the extent that she once refused to wear a red coat during the election!) had lost their appeal. This applied to her brother as much as it did to her. Jack in fact became a member of the Communist Party, a step Naomi never felt able to take, though she struggled doggedly through *Das Kapital* in the late twenties. 'It was all rather remote, not only from my comfortable London life, but still more from fifth-century Athens or wherever else my imagination happened to be.'

The General Strike of 1926 found both Dick and Naomi Mitchison unsure of their political affiliations. 'Of course a lot of my friends were doing lovely things like driving trains that we'd all wanted to do when we were children. At the same time, I did feel that the miners had been badly treated and was vaguely on their side. My father supported the Samuel Report, though he didn't agree with everything the miners were doing. And then of course, the press was against the strikers, and one can't help being affected by that . . .'

Nonetheless, they did become more involved with left-wing politics, their friendship with Douglas and Margaret Cole (she was the moving spirit of the Fabian Society) eventually bringing Dick into the Labour Party and taking the ailing Douglas Cole's place as candidate for Kings Norton in the 1931 election. It was at this point that Naomi too joined the Labour Party. Though he was not to win a seat until 1945, the next fourteen years were to teach Naomi a lot about constituency work and the political situation in general.

'I was beginning to see what was happening to ordinary people during the depression, before the days of Beveridge, when there was no social security and one realised there was a terrible injustice going on . . . I wasn't feeling very political when Dick was adopted as a candidate, but then I got swept into the Labour movement, which was something very real and very powerful and very united at that time.'

Yet there were many ways she could fit politics into her other interests. She would write rousing pamphlets for Dick's campaigns (including some especially addressed to women). And in 1932 she travelled with the Fabian Society to the Soviet Union. Before leaving, Beatrice Webb asked her: 'What is the field of your investigation?' Archaeology and abortion, she shot back on the spur of the moment, and was stuck with it. 'I described the abortion which I rather reluctantly saw in *We Have Been Warned*. But the archaeology was wholly delightful. . . .' In a museum in Leningrad she got to caress a small bronze deer from the period of one of her novels. In fact her reservations about the Soviet Union are best expressed in a historical parallel she made: 'A lot of Sparta about all this.' She was sympathetic, but not converted.

In 1934, she made a sudden trip to Vienna to record the suppression of the socialists there by the Dollfuss government. *Vienna Diary*, the book which she had been commissioned to write from the material she collected, is curiously reminiscent of some people's accounts of contemporary Poland. It was when she returned from that trip and was immediately asked to speak at a Fabian Society meeting about her experiences that indignation turned her into a speaker as well as a writer. 'Before that, even speaking to a women's section had been absolute agony, but after Vienna, the ability came just like that.'

The year after, she travelled once more on the strength of her political interests. This time she went to the USA with Zita Baker (who later married Richard Crossman) and became involved in the sharecroppers' rights campaign. The two women offered the protection of their 'respectability' to marches and meetings, where on one occasion the chairman made the natural enough gesture of putting his hand on Naomi's shoulder while introducing her. 'I was a white woman, he a black man. Someone duly shot into his house, but luckily he was warned and under the bed.' It was here in Mississippi that she witnessed, for the first time, the reality of abject poverty.

'Looking back on that time,' she wrote in the third part of her autobiography, *You May Well Ask*, 'what I remember is the constant feeling that I was deeply one of the Second, Social Democrat, International, a European in brotherhood with European socialists: *Freundschaft und Freiheit*, we whispered to one another in the hurrying, anxious streets.' When she looks back at accounts like the one in *Vienna Diary*, she says, 'What astonishes me is the mildness of the "atrocities" which upset me and all of us so much, and the general amiability of the police. The sides have hardened since then.'

The sides were already hardening as the thirties drew on, however, with the Spanish Civil War and the rise of Nazism. Once more, world war seemed imminent. Naomi became involved with Tom Harrisson's Mass Observation experiment, one of the many who collected data about their everyday lives and experiences, their thoughts as the European crisis deepened and war was finally declared with Germany. In 1937, Dick Mitchison bought a house and some land up at Carradale in Scotland, and with the onset of war, Naomi gave up her London base and retreated back to the land of her forebears, to become mother to an ever-growing family of refugees and evacuees, as well as to her own children.

The Second World War, then, was lived very much on a day-to-day, survival basis. Naomi learned about farming and developed her early talents for animal husbandry. 'I worked a pair of horses and later a tractor – it's a nice little Fordson, the only engine I've ever been perfectly at home with and either you hit it with a hammer or you put a hairpin into it, and then it would start again!'

At first, she was rather unwilling to go back to a landowning position (her family having been landowners, and her politics having now departed somewhat from theirs), but she gradually 'became entangled' in spite of herself. She was 'almost forced into a semi-feudal position', so that she soon became 'as much part of Carradale as, say, the Post Office, and as much used by the community, collaborating with them in all ways'.

And naturally she became interested in Scottish nationalism and the preservation of local culture. During the forties and fifties, she was weaving Scotland into her writing, with novels like *The Bull Calves*, *The Big House* and *Lobsters on the Agenda*. She also wrote poems and songs especially for the local community. I asked her what qualities she still hoped to see developed in Scotland.

'I think possibly a kind of genuine democracy, something that can only develop in a community that has had a bit of a struggle to become itself. Of course it's interesting to be part of a movement which has had to shake off a terrible lot of second-rate values and to be genuine about Scotland.'

Dick's political career finally took off after the war, when in 1945 he was adopted by the Kettering and Corby constituency, and became a Labour MP. Once again, Naomi's talent for getting to know people, and her insatiable curiosity about their lives, stood her in good stead as a politician's wife. Dick, too, was concerned with the most down-to-earth aspects of his constituents' lives.

'He became a model backbencher, tremendously involved with local affairs and always encouraging people. He knew every electrical system, water system, drainage system in the place . . .'

Naomi meanwhile was not confining herself to being the support system for her husband's political career. Having once stood for parliament herself (in the admittedly unwinnable seat of the Scottish Universities Constituency), she turned her attention to local government, and was elected to the Argyll County Council in 1947. There she fought for things like improvements in the local fishing harbour and better roads. This work led, in 1966, to her being invited on to the Highland and Island Advisory Panel.

'I was on the Fisheries Group, because that was the thing I knew most about. We went all over the islands and I'd get involved in all sorts of strange ways with the islanders. For example, there is a very strong Free Church influence which is against any form of secular enjoyment such as can be got out of village halls. So I'd be talking to people about their harbour, and possible improvements on it, then we'd walk away and someone from the village would drop behind and whisper to me "How do we get a village hall?"'

Politics, says Naomi Mitchison, used to be a much nicer affair before the advent of mass television coverage and advertising. She speaks with great indignation about the 1983 election – 'of course I'm far from the sources of power, but as Auden once said, all I have is a voice to undo a folded lie, and there are a lot of well-folded lies going around now, being fed to us through the use of advertising.'

Though she would like to see Scotland have its own National Assembly with genuine financial power (and she recently wrote a pamphlet for the Fabian Society about oil in the Highlands), she was hardly surprised when the devolution referendum failed. The proposed assembly, she says, didn't go nearly far enough.

During the fifties and the sixties, Naomi Mitchison's literary standing went into something of a decline. It was the era of 'the angry young men, and they were definitely men rather than women. I think there was a bit of a bias against the kind of things I was interested in.' Nonetheless, she continued to write, often combining this with her travelling ('in the days when there was a decent amount of room on airplanes') and her home life in Scotland, where in any case her readership was much more constant than in England. 'I became much more consciously a Scot, with certain, perhaps I should say, moral values, which seem to have slipped away quite a bit further south.'

The travelling, however, always prevented her from becoming petrified into a home-body role at Carradale. 'A family is in a way a very stabilising thing, yet I always hated the idea of not being able to get away from time to time. There's something wonderful about being in a place by oneself, on one's own.'

It also kept her political interests fed, still. In 1952, having become involved with the movement against nuclear weapons and the Authors' World Peace Appeal (where she got to know, and quarrel in friendly fashion with, Doris Lessing) she travelled once more to the Soviet Union. Once again, though firmly against the Cold War, she declared herself 'no fellow traveller'.

In the late fifties, Naomi entered into a relationship that was to add yet another dimension to her overfilled life. At a British Council party, she met a young African tribal chief, and invited him to come and stay at Carradale, which was, in any case, always filled with visitors from all over the world. The young man, whose name was Linchwe, came back several times (during his holidays from the school where he had been sent in England) and eventually adopted her as his European mother – and by extension, as a tribal mother to his people, the Bakgatla of Botswana.

Thus, even with her own children growing up and leaving home, and her desire not to be turned into a matriarch, Naomi still couldn't quite evade the role. She took her new duties very seriously, travelling regularly to Botswana, being initiated into her peer group within that society. She acquired yet another perspective on the world – out of which, of course, several books were created, including *Return to the Fairy Hill* (published in 1966), which documents her relationship to this new family. 'If I could show the mechanics of a completely non-racial relationship, of mutual love between a Scots intellectual and an African tribe, I might help to solve a world problem.'

In her descriptions of Botswana she always uses the pronoun 'we'. She acts, she says, as a one-man citizens' advice bureau, helping with the filling in of complicated forms or providing contacts in the West for various purposes, such as education. She gives telling examples of two cultures existing side by side, sometimes in a remarkably harmonious manner.

'Take, for instance, my tribal granddaughter, Seingweng. She goes to the best school in Botswana, and has won the school science prize. Yet last summer, she also led her initiation group in learning many songs and dances which are symbolic of the tribe's history. She learned all this history herself, and feels that this gathering of girls and women must stand together – that they are all her sisters – and really, you can see that she already has a great sense of responsibility to these traditions.'

Currently, she is worrying about how Botswana, in common with many areas of Africa, will cope with the worsening drought brought about by climatic changes over the last couple of years. Closer to home, she also opposes the local US military base at Campbeltown. When a young American naval officer came to her house recently to ask if they might take a small collapsible boat across her land at Carradale Point as part of a NATO exercise, she gave him a long lecture about nuclear weapons and the like before telling him he could go ahead.

'I suppose he thought the Old Bag was nuts, but he appeared to listen politely. The deputation left and I went on furiously podding beans, wishing I could believe I had had some effect.'

And so, in her mid-eighties, she carries on with life as she always has done, slowed, perhaps, by the physical inconvenience of an ageing body, but not by much else that I could see. Dick Mitchison, who had been made a life peer in 1964 – thus bestowing on Naomi the formal title of Lady Mitchison, a title she is reluctant to use except perhaps as the thin end of a wedge against the pompous – died in 1970. Naomi, so far, remains: a survivor and an indefatigable explorer. When she turned 80, she made a small concession to her age: she stopped driving the tractor. But she still travels extensively, making regular trips to Botswana, visiting her children, grandchildren and great-grandchildren. And she still writes, having by now published over eighty books. I asked her what she had enjoyed most about her life.

'Satisfying my curiosity about everything,' she answered without hesitation. 'About people and plants, about beauty in all sorts of forms. And, I suppose, writing. I mean, I've had all sorts of pleasures and things in my life which people feel are more important, but the practice of one's skill is probably still the most satisfying thing that can happen to one.'

Writing, she says, is like being up in the air: 'Everything looks brighter and clearer and cleaner – but then if one could describe it properly, one could perhaps live it all the time.' Which she doesn't think would be advisable. 'You've got to keep one foot on the ground, always.' So she gardens, she cooks, she entertains, she goes fishing, she travels. She listens to other people's stories and weaves stories of her own. 'I'm a compulsive storyteller,' she says, 'I'm one of those old women who sit in a corner by the fire, and people come and sit on the ground in front of her and say, tell me another.'

Certainly, it is her keen eye and her descriptive ability that constitute her accomplishment, not only as a writer, but as a human being caught up in the issues and struggles of her time. Her ability to convey the qualities of her own sex is an important element in her work, be it fiction, travel or political writing. Her diary from the first trip to Russia, for instance, contains a delightful description of a young woman she met whilst by the sea in the Crimea:

'She was a physicist in Leningrad and was very beautiful. She was really terrified of war with other countries – it was obviously her nightmare: to see all the new lovely socialist things they had been building up destroyed by the awful people with teeth and claws and money and swastikas like on the posters. She asked me as we sat in the sun drying whether people in England didn't hate Russia and want to destroy it; I said I thought very few people wanted that and only because they were frightened and that many people were full of sympathy and goodwill. I do hope that's true; I believe it is . . . I asked her if she is going to have children and she said "Yes, yes, I have one now", looking with pride down on her beautiful golden body just softening a little into the new curves.'

Her fiction, whether it has been historical, contemporary, or more recently, science fantasy such as the highly entertaining *Memoirs of a Spacewoman*, is laced through with this same curiosity and sympathy for people in their many guises. In 1983, she published another (and very topical) science fantasy novel *Not By Bread Alone*, which deals with the attractions and perils of genetic engineering. Alongside the new writing has begun the reclamation of the old; Virago have reprinted her enormously long epic *The Corn King and the Spring Queen*. Though one novel draws on the near future and the other on the distant past, and though they were written over fifty years apart, the basic concern in both is the same. What are the cultural values that genuinely foster the quality of life, rather than simply pursuing a standard of living?

Naomi Mitchison feels that women, who 'have to be twice as strong as the equivalent man' if they're to succeed in fulfilling all the roles the modern world demands of them, are nonetheless born with particular strengths, even now. 'I think being a woman is a rather splendid thing.'

To my mind, Naomi Mitchison stands for a feminism that doesn't try to pass laws about what women should and shouldn't be doing. She professes herself unwilling to be co-opted by any doctrinaire political grouping, just as she once refused to be co-opted by communism. Only recently, I spotted a letter from her in *Green Line*, a small circulation magazine reflecting the interests of the British 'green' movement, where she argues for the ecological perspective that permits diversity to inform unity. 'We can't all wear the same hat,' she wrote. 'The good old Marxist cloth cap, even with Freudian and feminist trimming, doesn't become us all. Nor does it quite explain why yesterday's revolutionaries always turn into today's Puritans, eager to cut out all individualist human frailties.'

For Naomi Mitchison is nothing if not an individualist. She has refused to remould her social identity for the sake of her socialism, blending just a small suspicion of 'noblesse oblige' with her open-minded appreciation of her fellow human beings and their concerns. She is at once radical and traditionalist, focusing with regret on our alienation from the natural world of birth and death, sowing and reaping, the cycle of the seasons, yet realistically assessing the methods of modern medicine and agri-business as stemming from our desire to care for and feed ourselves more efficiently.

And yet, I suspect, it is the ecological and feminist utopian that gets the upper hand. Certainly she has never been one for succumbing to routine and mechanisation. 'Life is destroyed that way,' she wrote in her birth control pamphlet in 1930. Naomi Mitchison interests me particularly because of her dogged pursuit of concerns only recently made fashionable, and because of the realism which she brings to these concerns: a realism that comes perhaps from having witnessed the whole of this troubled century unfold. She *inspires* me, however, for the breadth and warmth of her personality; for her emotional honesty. These are the qualities that emerge so clearly in this poem, which is from the collection of short stories and verse published in 1933 and called *A Delicate Fire*. And that, I suppose, is what I perceive when I think of her writing: a delicate fire. A fire drawn directly from her life.

TWO MEN AT THE SALMON NETS

Outside, in the rain, on the edge of evening,
There are men netting salmon at the mouth of the Tweed.
Two men go out of the house to watch this thing,
Down the steep banks and field tracks to their minds' and
    bodies' need.

How can I, being a woman, write all that down?
How can I see the quiet pushing salmon against the net?
How can I see behind the sticks and pipe-smoke, the
    intent frown,
And the things speech cannot help with on which man's
    heart is set?

Must we be apart always, you watching the salmon nets,
    you in the rain,
Thinking of love or politics or what I don't know,

While I stay in with the children and books, and never
  again
Haul with the men on the fish-nets, or walking slow
Through the wet grass in fields where horses have lain,
Be as sure of my friends as I am of the long Tweed's flow?

Paule Vézelay

Paule Vézelay was born in 1892, the daughter of Patrick Watson-Williams. She was educated in Bristol; then studied painting and etching at the Bristol Municipal School of Art. In 1912 she moved to London, studying briefly at the Slade School and at the London School of Art. Her first one-woman exhibitions were in 1920 in Brussels and Paris; in 1926 she decided to live in Paris, and at this time changed her name to Paule Vézelay. She continued to paint and to show her work and had established a considerable reputation in the modern art movement when she was forced to return to England by the outbreak of the Second World War. Her most recent exhibition was at the Tate Gallery, London. Ronald Alley, Keeper of the Tate Gallery's Modern Collection, selected and catalogued the exhibition. Paule Vézelay was interviewed for the television series by Germaine Greer.

'I will paint something more beautiful than Nature. I will paint Nature herself more beautiful than she is. I will paint the spirit of Nature.' (1922)

'I think a painting or drawing wants to have air indicated.' (1983)

Paule Vézelay

'Can you hear the blackbird?' We had fallen silent, after I had asked Paule Vézelay if she ever painted whilst listening to music, and she answered no, she never did. Painting, she said, has a rhythm all its own. 'Though I suppose I could try it,' she said, musingly.

The silence which brought the blackbird to her attention was not the first to punctuate our conversation. By this stage I had grown used to them, in fact I rather liked them. I was staring at a particularly beautiful canvas hanging on Paule Vézelay's living-room wall, a formless composition which, like many of her more recent works, used colour and light in a fashion that, Turner-like, brought about an extraordinary quietness, an almost dream-like state in me as I looked at it.

I think I left that small house in Barnes having learned more from the paintings and sculptures in it than I had from the woman who created them. Earlier, I had been looking out of the window in her studio on to the garden at the back of her house, and I had seen what I suppose was that selfsame blackbird eating rosehips off a bush. The garden was in sharp contrast to the neighbouring patches of suburban neatness, with their well-tended lawns and borders. Over the wall at the end, I could see an ugly brick warehouse-style building with a flat roof. But the garden, with its large ferns, its holly bushes, its various trees and its tangle of undergrowth, held its own against the outside world pressing in upon it.

The studio in which I was standing was somewhat tidier than the garden. It had to be. Once again, the strange contrast between the suburban and the bohemian prevailed, for the room was definitely bedroom-sized, and could only just contain all the paintings that were stacked against the walls. Yet the light from the east-facing windows, and reflected back off the white walls of the room, was good. In the middle of the room was a small easel and chair, with Paule Vézelay's current work placed on it, a pastel in reddish-orange colours. At the top of the picture, the hot colours suddenly faded to blue.

The number of paintings that were actually hanging on the walls of the small room and the staircase that led up to it was minimal compared to the vast number frustratingly stacked one against the other – and for this reason, very hard to look at properly. I asked her if any books containing good colour reproductions of her work had ever been published. No, she said, looking almost surprised at the thought. I was torn between wanting to go on looking at one thing after another, and the knowledge that we should really go downstairs again so she could sit down and relax. She seemed particularly frail this morning, and confessed to me that she had had a bad night. Her large, almond-shaped eyes shone out of her small, slightly bowed face, at once inviting question and asking for discretion. Her mouth, with its rueful expression, confirmed the feeling.

On a shelf near the door there was an assortment of small sculptures, some of the three-dimensional 'Lines in Space' boxes for which she is so well known, and a photograph of herself in 1927, soon after she settled in Paris. It was a strong, serious, inscrutable face, framed in the geometry of short, black hair and the dramatically upturned collar of a winter coat. As we left the room, I couldn't resist stroking, with the tip of my finger, a small plaster cast for a bronze I had noticed downstairs. Vézelay noticed the gesture, and smiled as she turned to grip her stick and make her way towards the stairs.

Down in the sitting-room once more, we sat by the fire and talked. The well-cared-for, antique furniture and the pieces of Staffordshire pottery contrasted oddly with the modern paintings, sculptures and reliefs to be found everywhere, not only her own, but those of artists like Jean Arp, one of whose delightfully sensuous bronzes had greeted me on the upstairs landing earlier.

During the conversation that followed, and in everything I have read about Paule Vézelay, a curious paradox emerges. On the one hand, you are talking to a polite, somewhat reticent Englishwoman who informs you that her private life is very ordinary and that she'd rather not discuss it. On the other hand, you are bound to have *some* curiosity about her life, if only because you find yourself face to face with this fascinating character, this powerful creative spirit who at the age of ninety-one is still producing innovative, technically accomplished and inspiring work. John Russell Taylor, writing in *The Times* about the major retrospective of her work at the Tate Gallery in 1983, asked: '. . . of how many painters in their nineties can you seriously say you have no idea what they will do next?'

And so I find myself attempting to make a portrait of Paule Vézelay which follows the principles she herself follows in her work. Because she is not willing to divulge many details about her personal life and feelings (and this is, after all, her right), I shall use what sparse lines she and others have provided to try and express the essence of this remarkable woman and artist. This will be a portrait according to her own definition, enunciated in an article she wrote in 1922, and which is to all intents and purposes a manifesto.

'I will paint you men and women,' cried the modern artist, according to Vézelay, then just turning thirty, 'not as you see them in the streets or in the drawing-room – superficial resemblances – but as they really are to you, and to me: human beings, the true significance of which is not expressed in the drooping of a moustache or the tilting of an eyebrow.' ('Let Nothing Be Lost Upon You', *Drawing and Design* review, 1922.)

Suffice it, then, to say that the true significance of Paule Vézelay is not to be found in the intricacies of her personal relationships or what enmities and rivalries may have existed amongst her family, friends or colleagues. Indeed, in keeping certain areas of her life firmly out of the public arena ('I'm not ashamed of anything in my life, but I think it's scandalous to share it with the grocer on the corner'), she directly challenges the prurient interest in stereotyped behaviour patterns that modern journalism all too often substitutes for genuine interest in the individual woman and her unique achievements. Indeed, by turning aside questions that are out of harmony with her sense of self, she actually avoids the need for defensiveness. This said, I can nonetheless trace the principal lines of Paule Vézelay's life.

She was born in Clifton, Bristol, on the fourteenth of May 1892. Her father, Patrick Watson-Williams, was a leading ear, nose and throat specialist, and the family were well-to-do, respected members of the community. She describes her mother as 'someone who enjoyed life', and proceeds to describe the atmosphere of ease, with servants and parties, which prevailed during her childhood – 'very different from now, very different.' Her father was one of the first people in Bristol to own a car. On her mother's side she is distantly related to George Fox, founder of the Quaker movement. The philosopher F. H. Bradley, whose book *Appearance and Reality* appeared the year before she was born, was her great-uncle.

None of the immediate members of her family appear to have had any particular artistic gifts, except for her father, who used to draw his patients and illustrate his own medical books. When he went fishing, and the trout didn't rise, he would draw landscapes too, 'charming small landscapes, but maybe I'm biased'.

Vézelay was to all intents and purposes an ordinary child, 'good at games and gym, liked reading, no special brilliance apparent'. She liked playing hockey, tennis and cricket, and recalls the school had a special coach, a man from Clifton College, 'who taught us *proper* cricket'. She also, in her late teens, enjoyed being taught to drive by her father's chauffeur. She had an elder brother, a younger brother and two younger sisters, though she was never particularly close, she says, to any of them.

It was apparent from a fairly early age, however, that this otherwise ordinary little girl had a talent for drawing. During her teens, she took the Royal Drawing Society's exams every year, and consistently got a pass with honours. In her school, art was generally 'well-taught, practical and quite helpful'. She didn't decide to be an artist, she says now, she just knew she *was* one.

To some extent at least, her father encouraged her talent, allowing her to attend art school in Bristol at seventeen, where she got her first basic training in draughtsmanship in the life class. When, two years later, she arrived at the Slade in London to pursue her vocation further, she was shocked to be treated like a beginner all over again, and to be taught in a rigidly academic manner.

'They were very old-fashioned, I thought. They expected one to measure up how many times a man's head went into his body and all this nonsense, and I was bored to death. So I asked my father if I could go and study under George Belcher, who was then quite unknown, hadn't even got on to the staff at *Punch* yet; but I had seen his drawings to illustrate a book and they were sensitive and, to my mind, excellent. I knew I wanted to be his pupil. He had started a little school in Kensington with John Hassell – you probably don't remember him, but he was a very well-known poster artist at the time – and I went there and remained for two years until the war closed the school.'

This ability to decide for herself, quite often against the pre-vailing consensus (for the Slade had a very high reputation, of course), what she was looking for and what she needed for her own development, was to mark Vézelay's entire career. Firmly and quietly independent always, she knew before she turned twenty that she didn't want to be trained as a classical artist. The people at the Slade, she says, all 'drew more or less in the same way'.

Neither has she scorned the mastery of technique as such – indeed the critic J. P. Hodin has called her a 'master of classical abstraction'. 'It is well to remember,' wrote Vézelay in 1944, with the benefit of hindsight, 'that drawing and painting are sciences, sciences which have immutable laws of harmony and a technique which no amount of "genius" or "inspiration" finds ready to hand. Long years of study are necessary before an artist can hope to say, like an Old Master of China:

> "Our spirit must make our hand its servitor;
> Our hand must respond to each behest of the spirit."'

Vézelay strove particularly hard to become a master of line. 'A line's very extraordinary,' she told Germaine Greer. 'It can be dark, or light, or curved, or straight. It can be a lively line, it can be a dull line, but you've got to be able to control it with your hand and that takes years of practice.'

She was able to get this practice under George Belcher, who believed in using models found on the street rather than the usual professional models. Paule Vézelay became head of his class, and was put in charge of engaging and posing these models, who she says were fascinating to draw, even if 'they did sometimes smell rather strongly'. She won the Belcher scholarship, and the Sketch Club Prize. She studied the '100 best paintings' in London's museums and galleries, and took additional classes in lithography at Chelsea Polytechnic in the evenings, returning to sleep in a hostel, Queen Alexandra's House near the Albert Hall, where the lights were turned off from a main switch at ten o'clock, prompt, each night.

Then came the war. All her male colleagues at the London School of Art went off to fight – and few returned. Vézelay's two brothers, one of whom was a newly-qualified doctor at Ypres and the other of whom was gassed at the front when he was only eighteen, did by some miracle survive, though most families in Bristol lost a son. 'You can't imagine what it was like,' says Vézelay. 'A generation of young men was wiped right out of my life – we were told we should no longer expect to marry.'

To the war, and to the fact that she never subsequently met 'what my nurse would have called Mr Rightman', she puts down the fact that she never did marry. Though she also admits it would have been hard to pursue both marriage and career. 'I should have liked to have a baby, though. I like babies.' Vieira da Silva, one of the artists with whom she was friendly in the twenties and thirties in Paris, recalls Vézelay once giving her some 'very useful feminist advice'. Beautiful women, said Vézelay, tended to get married and have children, and then they are unable to work properly as artists.

Whatever Vézelay's feelings about the war, she nonetheless tried to play her part. She wanted to volunteer as a nurse, but the fact that she was an art student seemed to count against her, and there was already a long list of girls waiting to be trained. So she went to work for the Red Cross, making papier-mâché prosthetic devices for the returning wounded.

Meanwhile, she also continued to draw, putting the lithographic training she had squeezed in with the Chelsea Polytechnic to good use, developing a strong graphic style in her black and white illustrations. Her first commercial success came when her illustrations for the anonymous and satirical *A Diary of the Great Warr by Saml. Pepys, Junr.* were published by John Lane in 1916, and quickly went to seven editions.

For the next few years she was to establish a reputation as an illustrator, lithographer and wood engraver, having not yet turned in earnest to painting. In the last two years of the war, she wrote and illustrated six articles for *Drawing and Design*. The first one, entitled 'Black and White', set out the programme Vézelay was undertaking, studying 'the work of all great artists, paintings, miniatures, prints of every description, to learn a secret from each. . . . Every artist should see as many good plays, hear as much good music, and read as many interesting books as possible. Above all, each should know as much as possible of all classes, all sorts and conditions of people; knowing them "inside and out"; and be able to sympathise with them so that it is possible to laugh with the gay and mourn with the sorrowful; saying fearlessly, like Sarah Bernhardt: "I resolved to live. I resolved to be the great artiste that I longed to be."'

Vézelay was to return to this theme of the life-force within artistic aspiration. It strikes me as being more or less her fundamental manifesto, a cry of defiance against any influence which would stand in her way as an artist and as a woman determined to explore the whole of life with an unflinching eye and with genuine enjoyment. Her ability to translate her observations about her environment and her fellow human beings, not only into visual art but into words as well, is apparent in the next five articles that *Drawing and Design* published.

These dealt with London as she experienced it in 1917 and 1918. She wrote about the theatre, shopping (two women discussing fashion in the face of war-time austerity), air-raids (with brilliantly witty drawings), railway stations (the most solemn and telling of her articles or illustrations where the psychological suffering caused by the war was concerned) and music.

Then in 1918, she exhibited an early painting and two drawings at the New English Art Club. Two years later, she was to have her first one-woman exhibition, at the *Galerie Georges Giroux* in Brussels. That year, she also visited Paris for the first time. This proved to be a decisive turning point in her life.

She was beginning to find the post-war artistic atmosphere in England rather constricting. 'English art then bored me almost to tears. There wasn't anything outstanding to my mind at that time in England.' She felt there may have been a lack of encouragement for original work. 'The English don't like originality very much in art, you know.' Thus she gravitated increasingly towards Paris, the fascination of which she described in the article 'Let Nothing Be Lost Upon You'.

'Below my open window lies Paris . . . Paris, who draws to her side at one time or another every artist of the world. What artist who ever spoiled clean canvas can escape her allure, and who among them all can explain her fascination?'

Later on she goes some way towards explaining it herself: 'Perhaps it is a sort of "spirit" influence which is created like a wireless apparatus among the artists themselves.' Paris, she says, 'opens her arms to them all rather treacherously', as they pursue a ritual reminiscent of courtly love in the Middle Ages, whereby they make their offerings to her without hope of return, and if they are very lucky, the discerning goddess will show them favour.

Eventually, Vézelay would be drawn to uproot herself and take up full-time residence in Paris. In the meantime, however, her career progressed steadily in England. In 1921 she had her first London exhibition at the Dorien Leigh Galleries, showing her early paintings as well as drawings, lithographs and woodcuts. Most of her paintings in the early twenties still took people as their subjects, in hotels and cafés, theatres and circuses, like the Cirque Medrano in Paris where she went behind the scenes to draw the tightrope-walking women portrayed in *Elenora and Dolly in their Dressing Room* (1924). 'One imagines her watching them dancing on those lines in space,' wrote Sarah Wilson of the Courtauld Institute in *Artscribe* in 1983, 'pondering the precariousness of life and her future career.'

In 1922, she became a member of the London Group, and her enthusiasm for modern art led her in 1925 to organise an exhibition of contemporary painting, pottery and sculpture at the Lefevre Galleries in London (where previously mostly French art had been shown), with work by artists such as David Jones, Jacob Epstein, Paul Nash and Ben Nicholson. And yet, as she had written in 1922, 'outside Paris, it is hardly an exaggeration to say that Modern Art is treated more harshly than the illegitimate child.' And so, in 1926, she finally moved over the Channel, took up the name we now know her under and became one of the many artists in exile who enriched Paris during the twenties and thirties.

The question of the name change is not an easy one to discuss with Paule Vézelay. She was neither pretending to be French, she says, having always felt quintessentially English, nor was she wanting to pass as a man with the name Paul (slightly feminised by adding an 'e' on to the end), although she declares that 'it would certainly have been easier for me as an artist if I had been a man'. What is certain is that the name M. Watson-Williams, under which she had exhibited until her move to Paris, didn't really *go* with the work she started doing after she got there. Becoming Paule Vézelay (the surname coming from a town in France that she liked) was in some sense becoming fully herself – the self she chose to be, an artist working in the Paris School, a modern artist, a woman, perhaps, in a world dominated by male names but where she felt she could make a mark in her own right. 'What is important,' she insists, 'is the work – is it original, is it well done, is it good? That's what matters.'

And her work, whilst bearing witness to careful study of other people's work, was and still is original. She experimented tirelessly with style, moving from figurative painting to an increasingly 'abstract' use of lines and forms in her painting. Though abstract is not a word she finds terribly useful.

'I don't know who invented the word, a painting can't be abstract. It can be composed with lines and colours and forms, that doesn't make it abstract.' In 'Let Nothing Be Lost Upon You', she had written that modern art must aspire to portray 'life itself and all the emotions of life', and 'the *spirit* of things seen and understood, rather than the things themselves'. Paris provided a unique ambiance in which she could explore this principle for herself, where she could make her manifesto into fact.

'In Paris,' she had stated in that same article, 'by people who

43

should know of these things, [modern art] is regarded as likely, if wedded with sincerity, to give birth to everything of value in the art of the future.' Over the next decade, Paule Vézelay pursued this path with great sincerity. She also made some lasting friendships amongst her colleagues in Paris.

Two artists she became particularly close to, in the early thirties, were Jean Arp and his wife Sophie Tauber-Arp. She originally met Arp at a party. 'The host said: "Who knows Arp's work?" Of course this was years ago, and he was almost unknown. I said: "I do, teacher." So Arp said, "That's very nice, come and meet my wife and have lunch with us."'

It was the beginning of a friendship that lasted until Arp's death in 1966. Vézelay visited the couple frequently in their house at Meudon. She was immediately inspired by Arp's work, being 'astonished to see such marvellous forms' in his studio. In 1939, she wrote a poem about her response, which ended with the lines:

> Voluptuous volumes!
> Castles of rejoicing
> Where sensibility
> And passions meet
> To dwell untrammelled.

When asked in 1968 by the British art critic Charles Spencer to list the artists that have most influenced her, she mentioned Seurat, Etruscan sculpture – and Arp. In 1949 she wrote an article in homage to Arp which shows very clearly the effect his work had on her in this crucial period of her development. Yet the French critic Michel Seuphor (who is a staunch supporter of Vézelay's work) stresses that she in turn influenced Arp's work. At least one of his sculptures is like a reply to an early sculpture of hers, which she had given him.

Vézelay also became very close to Sophie Tauber-Arp, who had a studio above her husband's (though Seuphor, for instance, did not know for a long time that she was also an artist). Vézelay regards her as in many ways a better artist than Mondrian.

'She would have had more recognition if she hadn't been married to Arp. Arp was good company, he was very gifted. People came to see Arp, they didn't come to see her, but she was very gifted too. She was very modest – a very nice woman – *gentille*. She said: "How can I be an artist with one hand in the kitchen and one hand in the studio?"'

Paule Vézelay was also associated with the surrealist painter

André Masson, though she denies that either of them had any influence on one another's work. Some critics have discerned the presence of a Masson-like 'écriture' in her paintings. But who can say if this would have been said if the two artists were not known to have had a personal connection?

In Paris, says Vézelay, you met people in cafés, where one could sit for hours and drink in the passing scene. Thus, in a casual sense, she had contact with many of the well-known artists of the time – Picasso, Matisse, Braque (whose work she particularly liked), Kandinsky, and so on. The number of artists living in Paris during this fertile period was very high. Vézelay counts up to seventeen different nationalities amongst her colleagues in Paris during the thirties. Soon after her arrival, for instance, she wrote a piece for *Artwork* magazine about Juan Gris, the Spanish painter who died in 1927 at the age of thirty-nine.

Life was by no means easy for those who congregated in the cafés and salons to try and carve out a place for themselves in this hothouse atmosphere. Vézelay wonders, for instance, how a painter like Matisse, who hardly sold anything until he was around forty, managed to survive. She herself had an allowance of about £200 a year from her father, and paid around £40 a year for her small studio, with working materials, food, clothing, heating and lighting – never mind travelling to England and the small pleasures of life – coming out of the balance. Yet though 'I lived very poor', Vézelay remembers this time as one of the best in her life. She was free of family or housework. Everything was geared to her work. 'To buy materials, all I had to do was cross the road. Here in London, I have to go all the way up to Soho – and even then they may not have what I want in stock.'

She was also exhibiting successfully. From 1929 to 1937, she exhibited regularly at the *Salon des Surindépendents*, a salon where there was no jury, and which marked her firmly as part of the Paris avant-garde. In 1930, she had a one-woman show at the *Galerie Vavin-Raspail* in Paris, and was included amongst the French surrealists in an exhibition at the Stedelijk Museum in Amsterdam. In 1932 her work was chosen for a representative exhibition of contemporary French art which was sent to Japan by the *Confédération des Artistes d'Avant-Garde Paris-Tokyo*.

During this whole period, Paule Vézelay was constantly pushing at the boundaries of her work, finding her own way through the mass of experimentation going on all around her.

She describes herself at this time as being 'deeply interested' in her own work, and proceeding very steadily with it. In 1928, she began her first truly 'abstract' work (a drawing which was lost during her exodus from Paris during the war).

In his introduction to the 1983 Tate Gallery retrospective, Ronald Alley writes that this tendency, after a vaguely cubist period, came into its own in 1929 and 1930: 'Whereas *Flags* of 1929 still has recognisable flags fluttering against a grey stormy sky, the shapes in *Curves and Circles* of the following year are impossible to identify, though the impression that they are floating in a cloudy atmospheric space still remains. . . . These pictures, in which a delicate poetic sensibility is allied with a gift for pictorial organisation, are among the most remarkable of all her works.'

By 1934, when she was invited to join the group *Abstraction-Création*, which had been founded by people like Arp to bring together non-figurative artists of all nationalities, her forms and colours had become much stronger and more clear-cut. Her exploration of lines and space, the contrast of forms, was now well into its stride.

After 1935, she extended this exploration into three dimensions, recreating some of the curving forms in her paintings and drawings in small sculptures, relief paintings and collage. The organic, or 'biomorphic', images recurring throughout her work, have earned her a reputation as a particularly 'feminine' artist. The British artist Paul Nash, writing a foreword to an exhibition of Vézelay's new work at the Lefevre Galleries in 1936, went so far as to praise her for not having 'that intractable "efficiency" of the mannish female artist. . . . Here are only sensibility, tact, and a gentle but firm persuasiveness.'

Around this time she was also beginning her 'Lines in Space' series of boxes with threads or wires strung inside them. 'Lines in nature,' she says, 'are not pinned down on two dimensions, and this is a space age. Lines should be *in* space.'

Her attitude to her own work has a strongly intellectual quality, as well as an intuitive one. She likes to think for a long time about what she is going to do, making rough drawings and only then going to the canvas when the concept has matured in her mind. Thus the experiments with style evolved, because 'the more you think about it, the more it changes'.

In 1937, Vézelay exhibited the first 'Lines in Space' series in her second exhibition at a small gallery run by Mme Jeanne Bucher in Paris. Being shown here has been described by another Paris contemporary of hers, Henri Goetz, as a kind of 'consecration' – a sign that one was accepted by the avant-garde. Vézelay describes Jeanne Bucher, who was to be a staunch friend until her death after the war, as a very interesting woman with a passion for art, though no capital whatsoever.

'She started her gallery in two attic rooms in the rue Notre Dame des Champs, then took a little gallery in Montparnasse which became quite famous.' When she first visited Vézelay's studio, she was not immediately taken with her work. 'But finally she accepted it and said "I'll give you an exhibition". I was, of course, very pleased. It was difficult to get an exhibition in a good gallery and I never paid anyone to show my work, but she was enthusiastic about art, she really loved it and she interested all kinds of people in young artists. She used to say she didn't have any special knowledge, but she had a kind of flair, you know.'

One of the people who came to see her first exhibition at the gallery in 1934 was Miró, who is often thought to have influenced Vézelay. Yet she was already well on in her development by this stage, so the influence might possibly have been the other way around. A similar thing occurs with the 'Lines in Space' constructions. Other artists were using this kind of structure after the war, yet Vézelay is seldom credited with her early experiments or named as an influence on younger artists. In some ways, this lack of acknowledgement has been the constant dampener, a somewhat discouraging factor, turning the strong independence of her youth into the proud isolation of the last half of her life.

And yet, before the Second World War, her position as an artist in the school of Paris with which she identified both in vision and now in name, seemed secure. In 1938 she exhibited with Kandinsky, Arp, Tauber-Arp, Seligmann and others in the *Galleria del Milione* in Milan, and was once more included in a major survey of abstract art at the Stedelijk Museum. In 1939, she was represented in the *Réalités Nouvelles* exhibition at the *Galerie Charpentier*. She was working well and receiving the recognition she deserved. The outbreak of war in September of that year was therefore a particularly untimely interruption. Things were never to be the same for her again.

With the advance of the Germans, she had to pack up all her possessions and leave France. She had just redecorated her studio when she had to give it up, and was the last British expatriate to leave, in fact. She made arrangements for her paintings and furniture to be kept for her in Paris. She returned

47

home with practically nothing to show for her last thirteen years' work.

Back in England, she spent the war with her parents in Bristol. Nothing could have been more different from the existence she had grown used to in Paris. 'My mother wasn't at all interested in art, my father was; but I had to look after both of them as well as I could for various periods. It wasn't at all an easy time for me. We had these terrible air raids, and it was very difficult to work. But it brought home to me how courageous the English are. I remember one local woman, after a particularly bad night, saying "Such cheek, bombing the English, such cheek!" The worst things were those awful doodlebug bombs, which came down silently and then exploded. I thought I might die several times . . . I think we were all very frightened, but nobody showed it of course.'

Once again, as in the first war, Paule Vézelay wanted to make herself useful. This time it was her age that prevented her joining one of the women's services like the Wrens (in the previous war there had been no such opportunities). 'I tried to form a Home Guard,' she told Virginia Pitts Rembert in an interview for the US-based *Arts Magazine* in 1980, 'but got nothing but discouragement. One of the old colonels said he'd rather be dead than firing from behind a muslin curtain.'

Still, she thought, women could be of some use, and organised a group, ranging from housewives to factory girls, to learn first aid, signalling, even throwing false grenades Vézelay had designed to be the proper size and weight. Her artistic talents eventually found a more appropriate outlet when she decided to make sketches of the bomb damage. In order to do this, she needed a special permit. 'You couldn't just stand in the street and draw. A policeman would come up to you and ask to see your permit, and if you didn't have one, he could take your sketch-book away. So I went to see Kenneth Clark, who was director of the National Gallery, and he immediately said, "I know your work, of course you can have a permit."'

She was never, however, made an official war artist. They had all been chosen while she was still in France. But the War Artists' Advisory Committee (of which Clark was also the Chairman) did buy one of her drawings in 1941 and gave it to the Bristol City Art Gallery. She also sold sketches of bomb damage to the Bristol Museum. By 1942, she was able to combine her interest in the women's services with her work, when she started making studies of the barrage balloon centre outside Bristol.

Despite the cold conditions, and the occasional danger to the women who held the huge, billowing balloons as they were inflated – 'one silly girl held on too long and was carried up, falling back on to the concrete' – this work was one of the more enjoyable experiences of the war. Her drawings had gone back to being representational as opposed to abstract (though she also did a few abstract pieces during this period). The balloons were a fascinating subject to her, looking like 'a monster coming to life' as they filled with air, and allowing her to continue with her theme of forms floating in space, though in a non-abstract manner this time. 'I think a painting or a drawing wants to have air indicated.'

Yet the dreaded enemy of the artist that she had assiduously avoided in Paris, domestic duties, caught up with her during the war and severely reduced her time for creative activity. She looked after her parents and helped her mother in turn house and feed Belgian refugees. She regrets not having been made an official war artist, she says, because then at least she would have been paid for doing the work she really wanted to do. And, one might add, the status of recognition would have legitimised her need to do that work.

Towards the end of the war she moved up to London, where she had an exhibition at the Lefevre Galleries in October 1942. She was fifty years old, and at this mid-point in her life, she wrote in the foreword to the gallery's catalogue that art, catching up with writing, poetry and music, had at last freed itself from the mere imitation of nature. 'Having found this new freedom, some at least will go forward to explore the exciting but terrifying Forest of the Future; there, in spite of giants and dragons, they *must find their own way* to express those things which words and sound fail to utter. This, surely, is the artist's work and his *raison d'être*.'

And once again she drew on the example of ancient Chinese art discussed in a favourite book, Fauré's *History of Art*. 'Like those Chinese colleagues many centuries ago, they too will "awaken intimate and vague sensations impossible to seize, but of a limitless profundity; their disciplined liberty will enable them to express abstractions of sentiment merely by respecting the laws of harmony . . ." That is my endeavour,' she concluded.

And yet the endeavour, it seemed, was still not truly appreciated in her home country. Although she was a member of the Artists' International Association from 1944–7, she never rejoined the London group. What she really wanted was to return to Paris. Yet when she finally arrived back in 1946, on the occasion of a new exhibition with Jeanne Bucher, the impact of her forcible exodus seven years earlier really came home to her. The people she had entrusted with her furniture and paintings (and whom she had paid to keep them throughout the war) had made off with most of her possessions, leaving behind only a few of the more abstract works. This was not the only blow.

'Paris was full of ghosts for me. So many of my friends and colleagues had gone back home or died. Then I couldn't get anywhere to live. The Americans had come over and bought up all the flats and studios. A tiny room would have cost me seven thousand pounds to buy, and I didn't have that kind of money. I didn't want to work in a hotel bedroom. Madame Bucher was very kind and let me stay for six months in a tiny room above her gallery. It was packed with masterpieces by Picasso and Braque and goodness knows who, all stacked against the wall, with me sleeping underneath.'

France had been through many changes, both politically and artistically, in the time she had been away. Henri Goetz says that abstraction as a tendency was incapable of expressing 'what was in the air'. The surrealists were much more prominent. Artists like Kandinsky and Tauber-Arp had died, others were forgotten. Vézelay, in some ways, was forgotten too. She found herself among younger artists who, says Goetz, imitated their older peers without evolving their individual abstract styles; most of them 'had been abstract for three months'. Exhibiting alongside them at the newly created *Salon des Réalités Nouvelles*, it looked as though Vézelay would have to begin building her reputation all over again. If she didn't like being treated like a 'débutante' when she went to the Slade at nineteen, she liked it even less now.

And so she returned to London, still unable to find anywhere she could afford to live in Paris and with, in any case, less and less incentive to stay on. Jeanne Bucher, who had been ill with cancer whilst Vézelay was staying with her, returned to her native Switzerland to die, and the gallery passed into other hands.

Vézelay was now very isolated. Somehow she never made the close contacts with British artists that she had made with French ones. There was no café-scene in London, and she found the art-world here much more formal, and somehow cliquey, than the one she was used to. As for the colleagues she did associate with, such as Paul Nash (who had been a patient of her father's), they were too scattered to see one another very often. Vézelay was by nature somewhat retiring when it came to a highly-organised social life, and the friends that she did see in London were usually without any interest in art whatsoever.

'It's a terrible thing, loneliness. I think it's the most painful thing one can have. I've known it. But if I've been isolated, it's my own fault, because I wanted to be free of social engagements, you know; they tie one down, you've got to invite people. I didn't want that sort of life at all, I haven't got the money, or time, or the energy, or the taste for it.'

Still, work continued to absorb her. 'It's the best thing when you're feeling down, work. A great cure for heartache.' She was exploring yet another medium: textile design. She started with designs for the *Société Industrielle de la Lys*, followed by designs for Metz of Amsterdam. Then, for about ten years, she designed for Heal's of London, and had several of her designs included in international exhibitions. She enjoyed this work, she says, because it involved making patterns for a flexible, flowing background. Some of the paintings she did in the fifties and sixties reflect what Ronald Alley calls the 'simple cut-out shapes in rigid repeat patterns' that she used in her textiles. Through this work, in 1949 she became a member of the British Society of Industrial Artists and Designers, and was elected a Fellow in 1958.

Though she no longer lived in Paris, she continued to go there and to exhibit in Paris galleries, such as the *Salon des Réalités Nouvelles*, which to some extent carried on the tradition of the *Abstraction-Création* group, and where she showed until 1951. Then in 1953, she joined the *Groupe Espace*, which was formed to promote collaboration between architects and abstract painters and sculptors.

'I was asked if I would be the British delegate for the group, and mount an exhibition in London. I said I didn't think it was going to be easy, but I'd try.'

She was right, it wasn't easy. None of the London dealers would show it, deeming this type of art too hard to sell. But a far more serious problem than the reluctance of the dealers was the reluctance of several of the more well-known British abstract artists, such as Henry Moore, to become part of the group as constituted by its Paris delegate, Paul Vézelay. It is hard to unravel exactly what went wrong here, and what the motives were, but there does seem to have been a distinct element of rivalry, with one man joining to get the names and addresses of other members of the group, so that he could form a new group himself. Eventually, in 1955, an exhibition was held, in the foyer of the Festival Hall, with French artists like Arp, Sonia Delaunay and Walter Gropius exhibiting alongside British artists like Ben Nicholson, Geoffrey Clarke and Vézelay herself.

One of the lesser-known British artists shown was Marlow Moss, a rather mysterious but very talented woman whose name has been linked with Mondrian. 'She told me that this was simply because she was his only student,' says Vézelay. Her description of Moss, who 'dressed like a boy, at a time when women didn't dream of wearing trousers', and was frequently seen with a woman companion, is intriguing. How many other women artists, apart from Vézelay, Moss and Tauber-Arp, have failed to go down in anything but the most obscure art-history footnotes, and then perhaps only because their names are linked with better known, male artists?

The difficulties encountered by Vézelay in mounting the 1955 exhibition (which received scant attention) and with the British branch of the *Groupe Espace* in general (of which she was elected President in 1957) were bitterly disappointing to her. Officially an exile during her time in Paris, she was in a way far more of an exile in her own country, unaccepted in the art-world, unappreciated as an artist in her own right and cut off from those who understood her, both in space and in time. Henri Goetz, who visited her at the time of the Festival Hall exhibition, says she told him sadly that she was completely unknown in her own country.

Her work was represented in the 1957 exhibition *50 Ans de Peinture Abstraite* at the *Galerie Creuze* in Paris, but following this was a period of about ten years when she lost interest in exhibiting. She says now that exhibitions just took up too much time and energy, and that they never sold anything. 'I've had twenty of them, so I have a right to have an opinion about them.' She simply continued to work, further developing the 'Lines in Space' series during the sixties, designing textiles and, in her painting, moving towards the formless compositions filled with colour and light that moved me so much when I first saw them.

Since 1968 she has once more begun to be exhibited. There was a major retrospective at the Grosvenor galleries in that year, at the Zabriskie Gallery in New York in 1980, and finally at the Tate in 1983. 'She turned to abstract art in the late nineteen-twenties,' writes Ronald Alley, keeper of the Modern Collection at the Tate, in conclusion to his introduction to the catalogue for this show, 'at a time when it was completely out of favour in Britain and when artists like Ben Nicholson and Barbara Hepworth [who incidentally later also used wire in the way Vézelay had done] were still working in figurative styles; and she was one of the first British artists to commit themselves totally and irrevocably to the abstract movement.'

In many ways, Vézelay seems happy to work on in her small house in Barnes without the clamour of widespread recognition, emptying her life just as she is emptying her paintings, creating space and light where other people put the psychological bric-à-brac accumulated in a lifetime of attachments and commitments. Unlike many surrealist painters, she is not exhibitionistic in any sense of the word, preferring to distil something universal from her experience, rather than portraying the particular and the limited. Where she has encountered limitation, it seems, she has simply turned her back on it and retreated to her studio.

Paule Vézelay still works nearly every day. 'I'm much happier when I'm working, though you can't go on for ever; you get stale and you get tired. You get too tired to work well.'

Technically, she has always been a very precise and careful painter, and the good condition of her early work shows this very clearly. Paul Nash, writing of her 'tact' in the 1936 catalogue, went on to say: 'I use the word "tact" to mean literally, touch; for these pictures, with few exceptions, appeal to me, as things first clearly seen and then felt with both delicacy and precision, in the actual process of painting.'

It is apparent from the amount of her own work crammed into her house that she has not sold very much over the years. 'I would rather be with it,' she says, looking around her with a half-smile on her face, 'than sell it very cheaply for the sake of selling it. I like my work. Strange as it may seem, I like my paintings, I like to keep them. I'm never in a hurry to sell them.'

The French poet Robert Desnos described Vézelay as an 'explorer in dangerous countries' and wondered if one day she would be given credit for having excavated this terrain. The lure of the unknown is certainly something that seems to have motivated Vézelay all through her life. 'Artists must try to reveal new values,' she has said, 'to provide something more than our "daily bread".' The piece she wrote about Arp in 1949 expresses her bold and joyful response in the face of the shifting cultural ground of the twentieth century.

'This is an age when almost every belief and tradition shakes and trembles piteously among the fragments of those which have already lost stability altogether. The only conviction that remains arrogantly unshaken, refusing to be alarmed by the mutual turmoil of any of us, is the idea that nothing can, or should, remain static.'

Both her work and her writing about art is full of this optimistic note. Quoting Rimbaud, she proclaimed in 1942 an exuberant destiny for herself as an artist:

> *J'ai tendu des cordes de clocher à clocher;*
> *Des guirlandes de fenêtre à fenêtre;*
> *Des chaînes d'or d'étoile à étoile, et je danse.*

> (Cords have I stretched from belltower to belltower;
> garlands I strung from window to window;
> with gold have I linked one star to another, and I dance.)

While I was talking to her, Vézelay motioned to a big book on the Russian constructivists that was lying on her coffee table. 'I really don't think we can learn much from them,' she said, shaking her head. 'It's all so ugly. There are so many beautiful things to paint, why make it ugly? I dislike sad art, there's enough real sadness in life. I think an artist should create something joyful, or happy, or pleasing . . . I hate the way they paint beautiful nude women these days, so that they look as if they'd been run over by a tram, you know?' She has reservations about some of Picasso's work for this reason.

Whilst abstracting from nature, Vézelay has still maintained that it is in nature, as opposed to the machine, that the artist should look for lessons in form and harmony. 'Look at the trees – how graceful they are – left alone and not pruned back,' she says, contemplating her own unruly garden. 'They're living things you see . . . each branch searches the light, and it gives them a beautiful, natural sort of beauty.'

Her anti-mechanistic stance was aptly described by Humphrey Jennings, who made one of the most telling tributes to her work: 'Paule Vézelay will be labelled abstract, but she has little in common with the friends of "functional" architecture, pretentious builders of worlds of light, decorators of uninhabitable "machines-to-live-in", who call themselves abstract painters.' And, he continued: 'She is, I would say, a contemplative artist. Her pictures sometimes remind me of those refreshing letters and diaries written by retiring people in the last century, recording their thoughts and emotions without apparent reference to the industrial pandemonium, the banging and the clattering of bridge-building and rail-roading, which we know to have been going on around them. There is a line from Mallarmé, which, I think, suits her well: *musicienne du silence.*' (Catalogue for 1949 exhibition at Lefevre Gallery).

And so I left her, keeping herself to herself in a silence broken only by the song of a blackbird, this woman whom our turbulent times have tried and not broken, have aroused, and affected and yet somehow left behind. In spite of appearing to have sacrificed everything for the sake of her art, Paule Vézelay declares that, ultimately, life is more important than art. Perhaps this is because of the relationship that, even in 1918, she perceived between the two.

'Great art is the essence of life, concentrated, preserved, and having a rare and precious flavour. Exquisitely set forth; more real than reality, more alive than life itself.'

Dora Russell

Dora Russell was born Dora Black in 1894, daughter of a civil servant. She read modern languages at Girton College, Cambridge, and was awarded First-Class Honours in 1915. She married Bertrand Russell in 1921. In 1927 the Russells opened Beacon Hill School, to put into practice their own ideas of what children's education should be. Dora's marriage to Bertrand was dissolved in 1934, but she continued to run the school until the first years of the war. All her life, Dora has been a champion of women's rights and an indefatigable worker for world peace. Publications include two volumes of autobiography, *The Tamarisk Tree* (vol. I 1975, vol. II 1980). *The Dora Russell Reader* (1983) is a selection of her writing over many years. She was interviewed for the television series by Bel Mooney.

'I am not concerned with the morals of convention or super-stition, but with the morals of experience.' (Hypatia, *1925*)

'The real riddle of the Sphinx, as far as the human species is concerned, is why, with a creative life instinct common to all species, the human male has been so neglectful and destructive of his own.' (The Religion of the Machine Age, *commissioned 1923, published 1983*)

The wind was howling around the old, well-proportioned white house, perched up on the hillside near the Cornish coastline, not far from Land's End. Pulling up my collar against the cold and the damp, I followed my friend round the side of the house towards the kitchen door.

'Are you sure that's the right door?' I yelled anxiously at her retreating back. 'What?' she returned over her shoulder. *'Are you sure . .'* But by this time she had knocked, and a well-wrapped figure had answered it. It obviously was the right door, leading into a far warmer and more homely environment than the one outside.

'Hello!' boomed an extraordinarily powerful voice across the noise of the weather. 'Isn't it a terrible day? Come in, come in. Welcome, both of you.'

This was my first meeting with Dora Russell. I had been taken to meet her by Dr Lynne Jones, a friend who was very active in the peace movement. Lynne had edited a book on women's peace actions, and Dora was writing the foreword for her, link-ing the current anti-war activities of women with those of her own generation. I myself had grown increasingly fascinated by this particular social and political current, and by the connections between the women's movement and issues like peace and ecology. I was spending a fair proportion of time talking to and writing about women who were motivated by or concerned with these things. And so I watched with fascination as these two strong and opinionated women, with nearly sixty years between them, exchanged views and experiences.

Actually, it was Dora who did most of the talking. When nearly four hours had flown by unnoticed, and we realised with a jolt that we mustn't take up any more of her time, she received our apologies with a good-humoured grin. 'No, no, once I get going there's no stopping me. Next time we'll have to get me to shut up so I can hear more about what you lot are up to,' she declared.

There was no denying, however, the fascination of talking to someone who had concerned herself with questions of feminism, the cold war, the environment and education throughout the whole of this century. As we walked around Dora Russell's comfortable, cluttered house with her (a house she has lived in, on and off, for over sixty years), looking at mementoes from decades of travelling and campaigning, pictures of the 1958 Women's Caravan for Peace which journeyed throughout both Eastern and Western Europe, pieces of china and other gifts from the women she met *en route*, mountains of books, pamphlets and other papers collected over the years, a sense of historical rootedness began to take hold of me. The fact that this kind of material doesn't currently get into the history books (let alone the media – who wants to read about women embracing one another across the ideological divide, when they can watch scenes of chaos and despair in Lebanon or Afghanistan?) only made it all the more interesting to me.

In a sense Dora Russell represents the voice in the desert that won't go away. Not that her voice, in a physical sense, isn't powerful. On the contrary, the very next time I saw her she was addressing a women's peace meeting in London, having firmly refused a microphone on the grounds that 'my voice, as I'm sure you can hear, is quite strong enough on its own'. It's just that this voice is in a minority, not only because of her uncompromising views, but because of her refusal to stop speaking out. She may not always be understood, but this doesn't make her change her tune. Nor does it dim the fundamental faith in her fellow human beings which is apparent throughout her life's work. It is this faith that makes her views a refreshing change in the current atmosphere of weary cynicism. I suspect that she has always embodied this optimistic quality for those who came into contact with her.

The Dora Russell of today appears in essence little changed from the young girl whose sympathetic and enquiring face stares out at me from the cover of the first volume of her autobiography, *The Tamarisk Tree*. The warm, slightly hooded brown eyes, the strong determined mouth that looks as though it might at any moment spread into one of those irreverent smiles, revealing just how deep those dimples beneath the cheek-bone actually go: all these things remain, along with the ever busy mind which has kept abreast of everything from philosophy to current affairs for so many years.

So far, Dora Russell has published two volumes of autobiography, taking her up to the early years of the Second World War, and when I met her she was working on the third. She was having something of a struggle, since the success of the first two, added to her memorable appearance in the film *Reds* in 1982 (where she sang the *Internationale* straight to the camera), had propelled her out of the relative obscurity to which she had been relegated since the 1930s. A new generation of feminists and peace activists flocked to her door to pay homage and to learn what they could of the recent history of these two powerful, yet often interrupted, movements. Dora received all comers with great kindness and generosity, but, she says, 'I really *must* get on with my book, otherwise the next part of the story will be lost.' Being reclaimed by a new audience has its satisfactions, especially after years of neglect. But suddenly finding, in your late eighties, that hosts of eager pilgrims are gravitating towards Land's End to make up for lost time can be a trifle disconcerting, not to mention wearing. (For one thing, she *hates* housework, she says.)

What then is the source of fascination for so many where Dora Russell is concerned? Is it merely her exuberant personality? Or perhaps her ability to record and communicate to posterity the complex and frequently baffling events of this unsettling age of ours? I think it is both these things, but it is also the sense that here is a woman who has fearlessly embraced the major public issues of her time, who has not separated her private life from her public persona, and who is therefore in touch in a way very few people are with the very heart of a period – that's to say with the human feelings, ideas, and strivings that informed this period and therefore characterise it. Dora Russell is, in the deepest possible sense of the word, a public-spirited woman.

She derived this trait, she says, from her father, Frederick Black, who worked his way up from a modest background and a job as a clerk, to a very distinguished position in the civil service (for which he was eventually knighted). She describes her father, to whom she was very close, as 'a public servant of the old school, of high integrity and scrupulous in every detail of his calling'. Dora's mother, Sarah Isabella Davisson, was also the daughter of a civil servant. The marriage, says Dora, was a harmonious one, though 'there was no question but that he was the boss'.

When she was six or seven, the family (there were three girls and a boy, of which Dora was the second eldest) moved from Thornton Heath, where she had been born on 3 April 1894, and took up residence in Sutton, Surrey. There Dora won a junior scholarship to Sutton High School for girls. She was a bright child, though she says she wasn't aware of this herself.

'The terrible thing about school was the intense competition to be top of the class. For years I had to fight another girl, who was a good friend of mine, and always managed to get to the top of the class just a few marks ahead of her.'

Her father was very proud of his favourite daughter, and encouraged her academic leanings, though she herself had other ideas: she wanted to go on the stage. This originated during stays with her Uncle Albie and Aunt Hattie during Christmas holidays (and in fact during her father's postings abroad she and the other Black children quite often stayed with one or another of their numerous relatives), when she was taken to the pantomime in London. It seems that the extrovert in Dora, which began with tomboyish feats like jumping off the summerhouse roof or riding her bicycle full tilt down steep hills, had to find an outlet one way or another. Though theatre was not, in the long run, to fulfil this function, her extroverted, dramatic leanings were to serve her well in the political causes she later embraced.

Pressed to go in for a scholarship at Girton in Cambridge, the seventeen-year-old Dora burst into tears as she received the telegrams of congratulation for succeeding. These, she was later to write in *The Tamarisk Tree*, 'were the signs of a growing, but half-conscious, desire to direct my own life'. The idea of training for the stage had to be abandoned in favour of the obviously sensible thing: to become a Cambridge bluestocking and pursue her studies in modern languages.

She says now that she 'wouldn't give up those three years for anything' – though she feels the academic emphasis of her education went counter to her imaginative side as a child and an adolescent.

'I would walk down to the sea and talk to the god of the sea, you know, all these things that children do with their imagination. I also had some secret refugees that I used to hide in the cupboard and go and talk to sometimes . . .'

She also had a passion for gardening.

'One of the most important things about me really is that I belong with nature. Basically, it wasn't right to educate me into having one of these high intellects, because I do think of us as being part of the natural world.'

As a child, her pets included doves that would come and take seeds of hemp out of her lips. These memories were later to inspire her own educational theories. But in the meantime, it was her other side which predominated, immersing her in Goethe and Voltaire, and sharpening the critical faculties which were soon to be turned on all the presuppositions she had grown up with. Indeed, through this process her divided self was to a large extent overcome, since her intellect was made to serve her instinct.

The first thing to crumble was the Church. She discovered, and joined, the Heretics, a society whose members had rejected 'authority in matters of religion and belief', and accepted 'only conviction by reasonable argument'. Opposition to authority in religion extended to the philosophy of idealism still taught by some in Cambridge. Dora would cycle off to Heretics meetings every Sunday with 'a most agreeable feeling of defiance and liberation'. These were held in the rooms of C. K. Ogden, the prime mover of the Heretics and eventually a lifelong friend.

Another cause she and her contemporaries at Girton began to talk a great deal about was the suffrage movement. 'Gradually the emancipation of women was becoming part of the general atmosphere – the *Zeitgeist*.' After all, her father believed in his daughter getting as good an education as her brother. She and her friends read books like H. G. Wells' *Ann Veronica* (for which he had had tremendous difficulty finding a publisher).

Nonetheless, they were still chaperoned every time they went to tea with a young man. Whilst choosing the younger dons (such as the elegant historian Eileen Power) made this somewhat less onerous, 'the awful thing was that sometimes the men found our chaperons more interesting than ourselves!' Dora was still wearing boned corsets with back lacings. Where pre-war women's fashions were concerned, she makes an interesting observation about the suffragettes, who 'were not ugly old harridans, but elegant, often beautiful women, whose long skirts and large hats must have been a fantastic hindrance in fighting with the police'.

When Dora went to Cambridge in 1912 an intellectual ferment was well under way, with old-fashioned metaphysics under attack for its religious assumptions by philosophers such as G. E. Moore and Bertrand Russell. Dora, who was soon to meet the latter in person, has never, however, agreed with his view that metaphysics henceforth ceased to have 'any bearing on practical affairs'.

'I believe,' she wrote, 'that the metaphysical discussions that went on in Cambridge from 1900 onwards had very great political and social repercussions, not the least of these the emancipation of women.' In fact, she has always held that ideas have as much effect on human history as material events, and was one of the first feminists to look to the power of these ideas, to clarify the roots of political and social issues.

During the summer which followed her second year at Girton, war broke out. Before returning to start her third year, she worked with the Women's Voluntary Corps in London, helping Belgian refugees – all too real, this time, in this suddenly serious adult world.

'Young and unpolitical as I was, this was my first experience of the meaning of war to ordinary, innocent people. I have never forgotten the tired, tear-stained faces of the children, the weary, haggard old women, the pathetic bundles of possessions tied up in big check tablecloths and bedcovers,' she wrote in *The Tamarisk Tree*. That tree, which stood outside her childhood home and symbolised her inner, fairytale world, was beginning 'to fade into the past as I looked into the now terrible reality of the present'.

Ironically, by robbing the young ladies of Girton of certain distractions, and 'speculations about the future', the war helped Dora to concentrate more fully on her studies. In the spring of 1915 she earned a first-class degree. She now found herself in a mood of indecision, not only as to what to do next, but as to the values she should embrace. Whilst her father held an important post in the Admiralty, several of her friends were conscientious objectors, following in the footsteps of men like Russell, who had spoken out against the war from the beginning. Dora still entertained thoughts of going on stage, and having suffered a near breakdown whilst at college, there was some doubt as to whether she was temperamentally suited to academic life.

Nonetheless, she was absorbed enough in eighteenth-century French thought and literature to decide to go and continue her studies, for a while, at University College, London, where she of course joined the Dramatic Society and spent many pleasurable hours in the British Museum reading room. It was during this period that she met H. G. Wells, who had been writing pro-war articles, denigrating conscientious objectors. Dora was so incensed by the tone of these (especially in a writer she admired) that she wrote him a letter in response, defending the courage and principles of the men who would not fight. He was intrigued by her letter, and issued a casual invitation to her to drop in and discuss it some time (he and his wife Jane lived outside London in Dunmow). This led to Dora actually walking there from Bishop's Stortford one snowy Sunday, having discovered there were no trains that would get her any closer, in order to take up his invitation – unannounced.

The pattern of this event is, to me, characteristic of Dora Russell, who never seems to have flinched from physical exertion or been stayed by questions of 'propriety' when it came to making contact with people who were doing things that interested her. She would be up and off to whatever she discerned as a possible source of insight into the world and its perplexities. Added to which, her defence of pacifists seems to have owed more to her unease at the attitude and assumptions which informed attacks on them, than to a doctrinaire alignment on her part with their politics. This is a trait which should, in my opinion, be borne in mind when attempting to grasp her later views on, say, the Soviet Union or sexual freedom. Her political development has always been informed by this personal, moral dimension which asks for patience and understanding for those that are 'other' than ourselves.

It was in the summer of that same year, 1916, that she first met Bertrand Russell in person. A close friend from Girton, Dot Wrinch (who was a mathematician and a keen follower of Russell's) invited her to go for a weekend walking tour with herself, Russell and his pupil Jean Nicod.

'We did the famous walk over the Surrey Downs, because Bertie wasn't allowed near the coast in case he signalled to the Germans or something, you see. I remember looking at his curious profile – it was so like the mad hatter, with his hair blowing in the wind. I think it was then I fell in love with him, really. Perhaps it was partly a father fixation I had, since he was quite a bit older than me. Anyway, he seemed to me one of the most wonderful people I had ever met.'

Dora came in for a certain amount of teasing from Russell, what with her family's naval connections. Laughingly admitting her admiration for the Navy, she realised that her attitude to the war was still ambivalent. But on the subject of her feelings about Russell, she was more decided.

'My conscious thought was of a man who must be much in need of sympathy and affection; he was being persecuted for his views and lonely, he had a gallantry that took chances and a spirit that tilted at windmills, both qualities which, in spite of better counsel, always compel my admiration. Neither then, nor later, was it the world-famous genius in Bertie Russell that I loved.'

The war was still dragging on when, in 1917, Dora's father, who was now Head of the Munitions Department, had to undertake a mission to the United States (who had just entered the war) in order to persuade the Americans to help the British Navy with their oil supplies. (When he had been Director of Navy Contracts under Winston Churchill, he had advised him about oil.) Since there was a certain risk from submarine activity, his secretary didn't want to accompany him, so he asked Dora to go instead, along with a school friend, as joint secretaries.

Given her growing pacifist leanings, she was not sure she ought to accept such an overt form of war-work. Visiting Bertrand Russell at his brother's house in London (on the walls of which someone had scrawled 'That fucking Peace Crank lives here' – 'a statement whose accuracy in every detail he considered beyond dispute'), Dora was encouraged to make the trip. Russell later told Dot Wrinch: 'She is not, like us, fully convinced about the war, but if she goes to America, she will find out what she really thinks.'

So she departed with her father on the S.S. *Lapland*, bound for New York. She was one of only four women on board (the other three were also with the British mission); very few women were crossing the Atlantic under wartime conditions. On the crossing she met a Captain in the Merchant Service who had been transferred to the Navy and had his ship blown up in the Mediterranean. He became her constant companion, and then, amidst a head of sailcloth on the top deck, her first lover. 'In wartime,' she wrote later, 'life was made for living.'

'I decided to get rid of my virginity before I was any older, you see,' is how she describes it now. 'I was after all risking my young life to get oil for the British Navy. It was a very patriotic thing to do.'

America was a very different world from home. In spite of the glamour and excitement of New York (a sharp contrast from war-torn Europe), Dora did begin to find out, as Russell had predicted, what she really thought.

'We'd always been led to suppose that the Americans were our dear cousins. They didn't seem like dear cousins at all. We were asking for help in our extremity, and there they were telling their own people they could use as much gasoline as they wanted. Every letter we addressed to the Government somehow found its way to the petroleum executive, which turned out to be Standard Oil. I realised that it was quite true what Socialists said about capitalists controlling government. Then I began to feel that, with the rapid growth of technology and wealth in America, they were quite likely to become an imperialist nation.'

Her impressions were not happy ones. She began to regret that America had entered the war at all, wondering what profit they hoped to get out of it. She disliked the crass materialism she discerned in everything, the flattery of the oil magnates who would whisper in her ear, 'little lady, what your father doesn't understand . . .', and tried to give her presents (which as a good civil servant she always refused). She began to feel defiantly European. When someone commented to her father that 'this young lady would give sixpence to a starving German', she responded that yes, she would, which was seen as a terrible *faux pas*. Yet she had a deep love of German literature, and had spent a year in Germany in preparation for studying the language and literature at Cambridge (and forming her first romantic attachment to a German boy she met there). The language of enmity, especially *vis-à-vis* people she had known and loved, was always utterly indigestible to Dora, whatever the political climate.

Now she wanted to return home to resume her research – and to share her experiences with Russell. As her father was about to replace Lord Northcliffe as Head of the War Mission, her mother was to come out bringing a replacement for Dora. She had heard that Russell was to be prosecuted for an anti-war article, and indeed shortly after she got back, he was sent to prison for six months – where he started writing *The Analysis of Mind*. Not being one of his inner circle at that time, she was not sure when, if ever, she would see him again.

The war came to an end. During the course of it, she was later to write, 'the clash between the new morality and the old had never been more manifest'. Incongruously, Dora was awarded the MBE for her services in the USA. But her views had now moved decidedly leftwards. Back at Cambridge, where Girton at last offered her a fellowship, she attacked Christianity through Ogden's *Cambridge Magazine*, in an article entitled 'The Right to be Happy'. Though in 1917, with ripples from the Russian Revolution reaching far and wide, it was politics, rather than religion, that were uppermost in people's minds.

At the same time, Dora was beginning to shape her life according to her beliefs in female emancipation and sexual freedom. She found a flat of her own in Bloomsbury where she could live when not up at Cambridge. There she could be her own woman, working and entertaining as she saw fit. Her lover at this time was a Belgian artist called Marcel, 'the true bohemian type, corduroy jacket, flowing tie, broad-brimmed black hat, beard and longish hair and all.'

Nonetheless, she was soon to re-establish contact with Bertrand Russell (about whom she had said to Marcel 'he is dangerous for me'). Invited to tea in the late spring of 1919 at the flat he shared with the pacifist Clifford Allen, she talked about America and politics, but especially about the role of women, marriage and children. She reiterated her disapproval of conventional marriage which she had mentioned to him the first time they had met. But she did eventually, she said, want to have children. She went on to assert that, along with the possibility of loving freely where they chose to, mothers should have a prior claim on children. Here lay, as she now puts it, 'the germ of our future differences'.

'He laughed and slapped his knee and said, whoever I have children with, it won't be you. And I nearly said, nobody asked you, Sir. Anyway, it was after that, that having gone to join a reading party at Lulworth for the summer holidays, he began writing letters to me. Then he came up to London and told me he couldn't do any work, and that I must come down to Lulworth. He sat on a little stool next to the divan – I still have that stool – and looked just like a leprechaun. I said I understood he already had a lady, and that I didn't poach. He said, oh that's all finished. So I took a risk and went down to Lulworth.'

Although this was a turning point (Russell had already started pressing her on the subject of possible marriage, should he divorce his first wife Alys), she was still set on independence and a career. In the autumn, she went over to Paris, having persuaded Girton that she could profitably pursue her researches in the *Bibliothèque Nationale*. She also still secretly nursed theatrical ambitions. Whilst in Paris, she not only continued to familiarise herself with the free-thinkers of eighteenth-century France, but also took voice training and attended some classes at Copeau's *Théâtre du Vieux Colombier*. And she started making notes for plays and musicals of her own, one of which contains a character who declared 'why, there's no discipline so hard as an irresistible impulse towards sincerity' – a line which suits Dora herself rather well.

For the discipline was to get even harder. Russell was still, in fact, seeing his previous lover Colette, who had refused to marry him and preferred to pursue the very same career that Dora herself hankered after – the stage. Dora went to see him in The Hague where he was meeting Wittgenstein (who, as an enemy alien, was not allowed into Britain).

'Bertie again pressed for a promise to marry, on which he would feel it worth while to seek a divorce.' He wanted children, he said, before he got much older. But Dora didn't see why she had to marry him in order to give him a child. She was, in fact, deliberately running the risk of pregnancy all this time. Then, on a holiday in Spain, he asked her to accompany him to the Soviet Union. And indeed she did want to see the results of the Revolution for herself – she had even started learning Russian.

This plan was overturned when Bertrand was invited instead to join an official Labour Party delegation to the USSR instead, in which Dora could not be included. Furious at the anticlimax after his eloquent speeches on the benefits of making a visit alone with him, she determined to get into the Soviet Union on her own, with the help of £100 Russell had given her just before he left (having said he didn't want lack of money to stand in the way of anything she might want to do).

As a matter of fact, nothing else was going to stand in her way, either. Travelling to Stockholm, she set about finding out how to proceed. It was very difficult to enter Russia in 1920, especially as an individual; the British government were against the visits, and the Soviets were cautious about issuing visas to foreigners who might be hostile. Eventually she came across Madge Newbold, a British communist also trying to get in, to attend the Third International Congress.

'What we had to do was book as tourists on the ship that went round the North Cape, in order to see the midsummer sun and all the rest of it. Then we had to go ashore at Vardö, which was a small fishing village, and wait. When we asked for the men we were supposed to meet, we were told they weren't there. Not knowing quite what to do, we started back to the boat, when they came up behind us and said, "good afternoon, Comrades". After that, they made all the arrangements, and we went over to Russia by fishing boat with a few others.'

They landed in Murmansk, where the local inhabitants were preparing to celebrate midsummer's eve. From there, they travelled to Leningrad (still at that time called Petrograd), on a ramshackle, run-down train. *En route*, a party of Red Army soldiers got on.

'When they found out there were two Englishwomen on board, they came rushing over, and a very interesting conversation started, with me trying to interpret in German, and them feeding us with tinned jam, which they said the British Expeditionary Force had kindly left behind. I learned all about the way in which the Revolution was supposed to happen on Marxist lines, something I knew very little about. One of them, a very attractive young man with fair hair, took off his badge and pinned it to my jumper. That was my experience of the wicked Red Army.'

One of the first people she met in Leningrad was the American journalist John Reed, who when he learned she had received her badge from a Red Army officer, laughingly commented, 'Oh! How brutal of him.' She was not, she said, afraid while she was in the Soviet Union, in spite of rumours outside of terrible events. Still relatively unpolitical, she did not think about any risks she might run, simply of her determination to be on the spot in person and see for herself. 'You could walk about the streets of Moscow in the middle of the night, and never be molested by anyone.'

In Moscow itself, to which she travelled next, she saw the anarchists Emma Goldman and Alexander Berkman, who were already somewhat disillusioned by the Revolution. But the most interesting person she encountered was Alexandra Kollontai, whom she describes as the finest woman she has ever met. 'She was the only Bolshevik who really knew what they were talking about. She saw very clearly what the position of women was, and that it would have to be changed.' Kollontai, who took Dora Russell to a congress of women at the Bolshoi, where many problems were aired, made a very deep impression.

'She was an unforgettable, graceful, inspired leader of women. One after the other, the women came to the platform to speak, with their young and eager, or old and gnarled faces, kerchiefs on their heads. And they spoke with the direct and simple warmth that I have now come to know in assemblies of women the world over, when, stirred by some common purpose, they open their mouths for the first time ever in public.'

Dora also caught sight of Lenin, when on her return journey via Leningrad, she was swept up and taken to where the Third International Conference was being held. 'He was right in the midst of a great crowd, singing the song of the exiles, and every now and then you would see his head popping up with his little pointed beard sticking out.'

Bertrand Russell, who had left the Soviet Union by the time Dora arrived there, was now back in London and anxious about her. Through the Quaker Relief Mission, he sent a message that he had been invited to go and teach in China, and wanted her to come with him. Laying aside her annoyance over the previous disappointment with him, she made (with some difficulty) plans to get home, travelling this time, not via the illegal route, but through Estonia and then on a Danish cargo ship to Gravesend.

She was now faced with yet another decision. Going to the University of Peking for a year with Russell would mean giving up her fellowship at Girton. 'My dilemma,' she later wrote, 'was no different from that which faces many women deeply in love, who none the less have aims, purposes, perhaps a career, of their own.' Yet within a few weeks of returning home, Dora was once more on her way across the world.

Described in this way, the decision might seem somewhat unrealistic. The full background is only really conveyed by Dora herself, in *The Tamarisk Tree*. This is because, as with many questions she has faced in her life, the decisions she has made and the allegiances she has forged are intimately bound up with the quality of her emotional life. 'I believe,' she wrote at the beginning of the second volume of autobiography, 'that an instinctive feeling of empathy for our fellow men and women resides in our organism, but is stifled by mis-education.' Not in her case, one might say.

The question of empathy was in a sense what divided her and Bertrand Russell on the question of the Soviet Union. The style of their visits there, and their responses to what they saw and heard, are in marked contrast. Bertrand, having travelled with an official group, was left with a feeling of uneasiness about communism undermining personal freedom. Like many others, he had his doubts about whether the Soviet system could be supported by believers in democracy – in other words, he drew a strictly political conclusion from the evidence his reason had provided for him.

Dora, on the other hand, had gone as an individual, without much security or any set plans, and had imbibed the spirit of revolutionary Russia. This didn't mean that she couldn't see the warts – confusion about the woman question, an almost religious dependence on propaganda over a trust in human reason, to name but two. But the experience had been profoundly different from her experience of the United States, which she saw as having succumbed to the god of industrial expansion, and thus having lost its soul, in some way. She felt that Marx had un-questioningly absorbed precisely the same materialist concept of economics as that which gave rise to the horrors of capitalism, and that the Russian Revolution's greatest hope lay in being 'splendid heretics to Marx', and not yet in the grip of the Machine.

Bertrand Russell made what was in a sense a quantitative political assessment of the Soviet Union, whereas Dora Russell made a *qualitative* one, based on her feeling for the organic substance of a people engaged in a struggle to survive in a world turned upside down. Hence her contention, to which she has held ever since, that the best way to let the more creative (as opposed to the mechanistic and repressive) traits of this society blossom is not to harass and threaten it. Her long opposition to the Cold War began with the view that it provided precisely the climatic conditions, as it were, to wither the seeds of worthwhile change, thus perpetually (and ironically) providing the material it needed to justify itself as a political and military strategy. Her views in this area, as in education, are not always easy to understand. From the point of view of a culture that assigns greater virtue to control than to trust or patience, she is open to misinterpretation, on the grounds of her spirited defence of Soviet attitudes. Personally, I think it is impossible to understand her unless one grasps that her critical eye is in a sense a maternal one, which posits love and a desire for the child to grow up healthy as its first premisses, rather than seeking to undermine or belittle the inexperienced being with its gaze. Her contrasting of 'The Soul of Russia and the Body of America' (the title of the first chapter for a book she began on the subject in 1921) goes deeper than either doctrinaire enthusiasm for communism or a crude assessment about standards of living.

'Communism has indeed shown itself as a severe impediment to the free flowering of the human imagination and intellect,' she wrote in *The Tamarisk Tree*. 'But, one must add, the cruel repression of ideas unacceptable to those in power in Russia may be seen as evidence that more respect is shown there for the power of thought to change the world than in countries where new ideas, published freely, are boosted as novelties and as rapidly cast aside, or merely looked upon by the powers that be as a means of permitting the dissident to let off steam.'

Of course Russia *has* succumbed to material solutions (albeit inefficient ones) and to domination by the machine, though on Dora's thesis that industrial materialism is a greater threat to freedom than any political ideology, and we may well have forced her to do this by refusing to let her play the world-affairs game on any other terms. And although the Chinese may not be proving immune to the disease, pre-revolutionary China did have an important influence on Dora Russell.

'The Russians still have this pie-in-the-sky idea, you know . . .

But the Chinese, I think, are almost the only people who know how to live on this planet. They don't believe in original sin, you see.'

The year in Peking was, on the whole, a very positive one, and not only because she liked the Chinese. Bertrand Russell and the 'very intellectual Miss Black', as the Chinese called her (also joking to British diplomats that their great philosopher had brought his favourite concubine), spent what Dora now describes as their happiest time together, setting up house in traditional Chinese style and becoming increasingly close. Then the cold winter resulted in Bertrand becoming dangerously ill with double pneumonia. But for Dora's care of him at this time, he might well have died. There were as yet no drugs to treat the illness, apart from a highly experimental serum which was finally used in desperation (provided, ironically, by the American hospital in Peking!). The months spent at his bedside willing him to live brought out Dora's most protective instincts.

'My feeling that he was not tough, but needed someone to watch over and cherish him, persisted [and this was even before he became ill] – a deep female pride that without us the male can never accomplish or survive.' There is a touching account in a letter she wrote to her mother, of how on her twenty-sixth birthday, having been told by the doctor that Bertrand was close to death, she held violets to his face: 'Every time he smelt them the delirium would leave him for a moment and he would cry.'

Then, as he came out of hospital to convalesce, Dora discovered that she was pregnant. This decided the father-to-be that they should definitely marry as soon as possible, an idea that Dora was still not terribly keen on. It is hard, however, to resist the urgent pleadings of a man who has been so close to death. Thus, soon after getting home and settling into a house in Chelsea (Bertrand's divorce having been finalised), the forthcoming heir was legitimised at Battersea Registry Office.

Once again, Dora had waived her principles for the sake of the man she loved. There she was, having taken a public stand on the issue of sexual freedom and a woman's right to have a child without any man asserting possession of either of them, doing precisely the opposite of what she had intended. Life, however, especially for those prone to empathy for other points of view, is like that. The American journalist Crystal Eastman, interviewing Dora a few years after her marriage, records her as saying that: 'Life isn't all earning your living. Unfortunately we fall in love and feminism must take that into consideration.'

For the next ten years, Dora was to combine married life with the social round, with politics and with children. Two years after John Conrad was born, she gave birth to a daughter, Kate. In the elections of 1922 and 1923, she supported Bertrand's campaign as Labour candidate for Chelsea. He had promised her that she would not have to 'grace the head of his table', but nonetheless most of his friends were older than her, and she would find herself playing a rather passive role amongst the formidable Bloomsbury set, whose talk was 'allusive, often learned, exchanges swift'.

It was difficult for Dora to create a professional sphere of her own where she would not be competing with her husband. In 1923, they collaborated on *The Prospects of Industrial Civilization* and Dora secured a contract to expand the ideas in *The Soul of Russia and the Body of America* into the full-length book, *The Religion of the Machine Age*. Yet in her thesis on the dangers of industrialisation, the male split between intellect and feeling, spirit and body, she was too far ahead of her time, and she received no encouragement, either from Bertrand or from any of her friends. Even Ogden didn't seem to grasp what she was trying to get at. This led to her abandoning the book, which she felt would have no audience, and writing *The Right to Be Happy* (published in 1927) instead. The machine age book was not to be taken up again until she was in her eighties, and criticism of the dark satanic mills of modern industry was at last being connected with the attitudes that perpetuate the cold war and seek to enslave and denigrate women down the ages. At which point, of course, one reviewer said that her contribution was 'nothing new'.

A book which did have great success was *Hypatia: or Woman and Knowledge*, published in 1925. This dealt with the sex-war, which Dora said women started out of sheer necessity, given men's refusal to allow them any control over their own lives whatsoever, whether it be the vote, or control over their bodies, or the right to support themselves economically.

Hypatia is a witty and brilliant piece of work (it was recently reprinted, along with other writings, in *The Dora Russell Reader*). Her empathetic eye sees through the tangle of emotions surrounding the issue of women's liberation, and answers criticisms such as the one that feminists are merely a new brand of puritan.

'They had need to be, perhaps, who in an atmosphere of swoons and ringlets, won for us schools and colleges, free limbs, health and the open air; unlocked for us the classics, science, medicine, the history of our world; drew us from our paltry, ladylike accomplishments; wrote upon our school-books: "Knowledge is now no more a fountain sealed", and flung wide the gate into the world.'

As a result of *Hypatia*'s success, she was offered a regular column in the Spanish newspaper *El Sol*, to write on any subject she chose, an opportunity she greatly relished. She kept this up for several years before pressure of other work forced her to stop. At least it showed she could be taken seriously in her own right, and not simply as Bertrand Russell's wife. In fact, the publisher of *Hypatia* insisted on issuing it under the name of Mrs Bertrand Russell, saying it would sell many more copies that way. Some libraries, says Dora, have even catalogued it as written by him!

Another sphere where Dora was able to carve out a distinct role for herself was politics. Although she had stood for Labour in 1934 (replacing Bertrand whose health prohibited a third campaign in so many years), and thus had the pleasure of using her vote for the first time by voting for herself, the main focus of her political work soon became the birth control campaign.

In 1923, she came to the defence of a booklet called *Family Limitation*, by the American birth control pioneer Margaret Sanger, which had been seized by the police whilst it was being sold in the streets to working women.

'Apparently the offending thing was a diagram which showed a finger putting a pessary into the right place in the vagina. It was explained to us that that might not have been the woman's finger and this was what was obscene! We replied it had never occurred to us that this might be a possibility . . .'

From that point onwards, Dora Russell campaigned tirelessly, enlisting the help of people like H. G. Wells and Julian Huxley, to make birth control advice available not simply to educated and leisured women, but to those who needed it most: working women, upon whom were inflicted a double burden of child care and outside work.

'That was my real education, when I started travelling all over the country to speak to working-class women, and I found out what their lives were really like. They would be back within the factory within days of dropping a baby, and there were all those other children to care for as well. . . . You realised what birth control really meant to them.'

Within the Labour Party, she and her fellow campaigners encountered some stiff opposition to their demands for birth control advice to be made an integral part of maternity care. She was told that 'sex should not be dragged into politics', and that she would 'split the party from top to bottom' (this from the Labour Woman Organiser!). Nonetheless the Labour Women's Conference of 1924 adopted an addendum on birth control in their maternity policy, and a group of women in the party duly formed the Workers' Birth Control Group (wanting to dissociate their work from anything to do with eugenics).

'The "Very Intellectual Miss Black",' wrote Dora in *The Tamarisk Tree*, 'now received her true political education. Feminist indeed, I began to wonder if the feminists had not been running away from the central issue of women's emancipation. Would women ever be truly free and equal with men until we had liberated mothers?'

Discerning that the issue went deeper than whether children were a good thing or not, into a deep-rooted contempt for women's bodies and a total undervaluing of the labour of motherhood (among other invisible contributions made to society by women), Dora and another woman coined a telling slogan: 'It is four times as dangerous to bear a child as to work in a mine, and mining is men's most dangerous trade.'

And in *Hypatia*, she suggested that 'though middle-class feminism has conquered the professions, the feminism of working mothers (could) bring a new and powerful contribution to our work'. She could not separate the misery of these women's lives ('bishops and generals like babies, landladies don't') from the spread of industrial and militaristic values.

'If Jason cannot give up his murderous playthings, let him have neither sons to destroy nor daughters to drag through misery. His children shall never be conceived. I have indicated that this is happening already, not as a deliberate revolt, but as a counsel of despair in a world which offers no hope, no joy, and no opportunity to the young.'

Her feminism was spreading through the rights of mothers to the rights of children. She and Bertrand had been spending holidays down at Carn Voel in Cornwall (the house where Dora still lives today) with the two children, and had frequently discussed the best way to educate them as they grew up. Disillusioned after the General Strike of 1926, Dora wondered about education as a basis for social change.

'We began to think there were more worthwhile things to be done in education than in narrow party politics. We didn't think that Labour was giving real content to education – but simply producing equipment and buildings. The children still weren't being taught in the right way. So we had the idea of starting our own school, because our children were getting to the age when they would need schooling anyhow.'

Thus, in 1927, they moved permanently out of London, rented Bertrand's brother's house in Sussex and Beacon Hill School came into existence. As one of the first progressive schools in Britain (A. S. Neill has called Dora Russell 'the only other educator'), Beacon Hill came in for a lot of bad publicity. The press dubbed it 'the go-as-you-please school' and circulated stories about nudity and lack of discipline.

The truth of the matter was that the Russells believed in the ability of children to set their own pace in life and regulate their own lives, in community with other children and adults, and that far saner and less violent human beings would result.

'You should look at a child and see what the child is interested in. You should provide it with the right environment, with liberty to explore ideas or physical surroundings, rather than constantly trying to drive things *into* the child.'

As at Summerhill, there was a School Council, on which all members of the school community, whether child or adult, had a voice, and it was through this that rules were enacted and applied. Dora agreed with Mao Tse-tung's principle of cooperation rather than competition in education, and expected each child to learn to take responsibility for his or her own interaction with fellow pupils.

'It's only in the twentieth century,' says Dora, 'that we've begun to think of not beating children, and to ask ourselves instead what goes on inside their heads.'

Soon after the school opened, Dora's book *The Right to be Happy* was published, both in Britain and the United States. This book sets out the fundamental premises of Dora's political position.

'I was saying that the basis of society should not be all these intellectual and economic abstractions, but should be biological. That is to say; what is a human being? What do human beings need for life? And I set it out, you see, things like food, shelter, some education, because curiosity is very strong, and then sex and parenthood. Then I examined how far our society really catered for these needs, and of course it didn't. . . . Everybody was talking about economic man in those days; I thought economic man was an absolute nonsense, and still do!'

The book was a success on both sides of the Atlantic, but

especially in the United States, where Dora went to lecture in the early part of 1928. Once again, her experience of this country was not very happy. She was both 'hyped' and attacked as an apostle of sexual freedom. She was pursued by Hearst reporters who tried to trap her into making sensational statements.

'I remarked that in England you might say what you liked,' she remembered later, 'as long as you *did* nothing, whereas in America, you might *do* as you wished provided you did not speak of it. People seemed to want me to be daring and outspoken and at the same time were scared if I was.'

Whilst in the United States she met an Irish-American journalist named Griffin Barry, who became her lover. He shared her feelings about the Soviet Union – in fact he had been there at the same time as her, having entered via Finland with John Reed. This relationship was to have far-reaching consequences on her life.

Though she and Bertrand Russell had agreed to leave one another free to have sexual relationships with other partners, Dora kept this side of her life separate from the family, whilst Bertrand upset her on several occasions (often when she had been away and he knew she had been seeing a lover) by conducting these relationships in their home. Once she returned to find the cook standing guard over the children, 'because, she said, the wicked man was sleeping with the governess, so she wasn't going to let either of them come near the children. I felt this was very unfair on me, because she was one of the first reliable cooks I had had, and I was very busy at the time, but I had to dismiss her. Though we looked at things in a different way, it would have been difficult for her to be with the "master" – which is what she called Bertie – after this.'

In *The Tamarisk Tree*, she observed that 'servants and staff played a bitter role in the story of our family, a fact which to me has some historical as well as personal importance.' She felt that the class basis of these relationships was liable to poison the atmosphere of the home.

Personal pain, however, didn't undermine her commitment to the cause of sexual freedom. She understood the word freedom to mean not rampant individualism (a disease which she felt plagued the West), but freedom in community: 'Freedom to behave like a human, a creative human being.' In *The Right to be Happy*, she had written: 'Love for our fellow-men would not have this quality of agonised repression if we ceased to feel that to be virtuous in giving to others, we were taking away from ourselves.'

Sex education, both for children and for adults, could not be divorced from a sense of organic continuity between one being and another, the search for harmonious outlets for our natural, animal instincts. To acknowledge our place in the animal kingdom was not to reduce ourselves to some anthropomorphic notion of mindless savagery, but simply to accept, with honesty and humility, our connection with the rest of the natural, physical world. It was this belief that underscored her opposition to religious teaching and the Church. 'I believe in a wholesome animal which is not sinful. The minute you begin to think there's something wrong about being an animal, you begin to think sex is wrong; that's what the early Fathers did.'

In 1929, after returning from a trip to the Soviet Union with Griffin Barry and a party of American visitors (with whom, once again, she felt ill at ease), both she and Bertrand participated in the World League of Sex Reform Congress, which Dora had been involved in setting up. Participants in the League were drawn from all over the world, including names like Havelock Ellis, Magnus Hirschfeld, Henri Barbusse, Alexandra Kollontai, the Huxleys. 'If anyone wishes to know who were the standard-bearers of progressive opinion,' she wrote, '. . . the index of participants is a reliable guide.'

It is perhaps ironic that whilst Dora was campaigning for a woman's right to choose whether or not to have a child, she and Bertrand had been trying, unsuccessfully, to have another child themselves. When she discovered that she was pregnant by Griffin Barry, it looked as if Dora's principles about mother-right would be put to the test. On the surface of it, Bertrand was perfectly happy about this, even insisting that this daughter, Harriet, should be registered as his child.

But the tide was turning as the Russells entered the thirties. Dora described this period as having a mood which not only affected politics, with a gradual ebbing of power from socialism as recession set in and large sections of the left started to regard radical experiments as a political liability, but also affected her personal life.

Her second trip to the Soviet Union had not induced the optimism of the first. Instead she was seized by a certain uneasiness which 'perhaps presaged the antagonisms and purges which were soon to occur there; I may also have become increasingly aware of how irreconcilable was my view of private and public morality with that still held by the majority at home.'

With the publication of Bertrand's book *Marriage and Morals*, with Dora's writing and campaigning becoming increasingly well known, and with their partnership in the school (which nonetheless, even when Dora later ran it alone, was always called 'Bertrand Russell's school' by outsiders!), they were regarded as an integral part of the progressive movement. Working together harmoniously in their daily lives, it was hard to see that anything could go wrong.

However, Bertrand, who on the death of his brother in 1931 had become the third Earl Russell, now became seriously involved with Margery Spence, a student from Oxford who had been looking after John and Kate. Once again, Dora felt usurped within her own home, but believing she had no claim of possession over her husband, she tried to make the best of the situation. In the summer of 1931, the two couples spent a holiday together with the three children at Hendaye in the Basque area of France.

And yet, as she was later to say, quoting from Yeats, if 'things fall apart, the centre cannot hold'. In 1932, Dora gave birth to a second child by Griffin Barry, a son this time, named Roderick. At the same time (in fact while she was in the nursing home giving birth) Bertrand left her and went to live with Margery Spence at their house in Cornwall. She now had to cope with a new baby, a school, and the trauma of divorce proceedings which dragged on over several years. This was especially painful in the light of the fact that Bertrand now appeared to retract from his 'progressive' stand, going back on the fundamental premisses on which Dora had thought their relationship was built.

In *The Tamarisk Tree*, Dora regretfully recalled this bitter time, when even Griffin Barry became enmeshed in traditional male attitudes.

'It was soon evident that the devastatingly possessive part of the creative impulse was parental emotion. A battle of "father right" versus "mother right" raged between Bertie, Griffin and me. The two men had decided that the obvious course was to divide the family in two according to their fathers; they also seemed to assert that "their needs", of which they spoke frequently, demanded the right to the children and the ministrations of one wife. I replied that, on the contrary, I had a family consisting of four children, and that quantitative values were irrelevant in the sense that "one is eternally the father or mother of a child, no matter how many one has". I refused to see John and Kate's lives chopped up to suit the patriarchal system.'

Her views on father and mother right were elaborated in her next book, *In Defence of Children*, which came out in the autumn of 1932, just after Bertrand had left the school. But in the climate of the time, the book did not do as well as her previous ones. Many people thought that with Bertrand Russell gone, the school had come to an end – and in fact, turning against it himself, he later insisted on John and Kate being sent to Dartington School instead.

Dora was nonetheless determined to carry on. She ran the school, through financial ups and downs, and several moves to different parts of the country, for another decade. She continued to attend meetings of progressive educationists, the Sex Reform League, the Independent Labour Party, and so on. The legal tangle required her to live apart from Barry (who had gone back to the USA), or indeed any other man, for two years before the divorce could be made final. It was a hard time, and she was utterly dispirited by Bertrand Russell's use of a social system on which she herself had never, when she originally married him, pretended to depend. His sexual infidelities (which turned out to have been far more numerous than hers) were not the issue, so much as his disloyalty to the intrinsic nature of their own relationship, based on mutual openness and work for the ideals they held in common.

'I was embittered because I perceived that he saw himself as conferring favours upon me and implied that, left to myself, I would not have achieved anything. He had forgotten that I had sacrificed a promising career and my economic independence to go with him to China, when his own future seemed precarious. I felt that he had never known what it was to have to make one's own way in life, to depend only on one's brains. Above all, he was allowing himself to be influenced by the old codes and had forgotten that once there had been an understanding and even a possibility of love between the parties concerned, and more especially for *all* the children. His defection from what I felt we had stood for had left me choked with a sense of failure in everything by which I had lived.'

She feels that if Russell had been faithful to her in the fundamental, emotional way she had been looking for (rather than paying lip-service to fashionable beliefs before simply scrapping them), they would have been able to stay together. The tragedy is that Dora was never destined to settle down in the kind of relationship she aspired to. In 1933, she fell in love with a young communist, Paul Gillard, who had come briefly to the school in order to help with secretarial work and write a novel. This could well have been the partner suited to her, but on 1 November 1933, he was found dead in his native Plymouth, and Dora's life was shattered once again. From this point on, she says, she lived only for impersonal ends, apart from love of close friends and children.

The mystery of Paul Gillard's death was clarified somewhat when, the following year, she met one of his friends, Pat Grace, who was convinced he had been murdered by local fascists (these had also daubed the school with graffiti whilst Paul had been there). Pat and Dora collected a substantial amount of evidence, but she never had the heart to pursue it through official channels.

Pat, who was homeless and jobless, now also came to work at the school. He became devoted to Dora and to the children, and remained her 'comrade in arms' until he died in 1949 from bronchitis and emphysema. In 1940 she married him, so that when he was called up, she could remain in touch with him, and if anything happened to him, she and the two younger children would have some claims on the army. Though they kept the school going until 1943 (repairing with a small number of pupils to Carn Voel when the war started and the War Office requisitioned their premises) bankruptcy and other pressures finally forced Dora to give it up and seek work in London.

Thus, from 1943 to 1950, she followed in her father's footsteps, working as a civil servant in the Ministry of Information. She started out in the Reference Division, and was then moved to the Soviet Relations Division and British Ally. She was once more in a position to be acknowledged by outsiders as a 'professional' woman, rather than an over-extended mother figure. 'I sat down and looked at the in-tray and thought how the devil am I going to endure this life, without any people? But before long I was right in the thick of it . . .'

She also remained right in the thick of politics, especially in the fifties, when she was a founding member of the Council for Civil Liberties, the Britain-China Friendship Association and an early campaigner for nuclear disarmament. It was not until the end of the decade that people from a wider political spectrum in the West became motivated on this issue, says Dora Russell. At the beginning of the fifties, it was mainly communists who took the initiative, and there were many who would not associate with them.

'For years I couldn't be a Labour Party member because I

1 & 2 *Naomi Mitchison (above) at home at Carradale House, 1983, (left) as a young girl*

3 *Naomi Mitchison, farmer*

5 *Naomi, tribal mother to the Bakgatla of Botswana*

4 *Opposite: Wyndham Lewis painted this portrait of Naomi in 1939*

6 & 7 *Paule Vézelay (above) at home in Barnes, 1983, (below) in Paris in 1926*

8 *Opposite (above): One of Paule Vézelay's pastels of barrage balloons. Executed at Bristol, 1942*

9 *Opposite (below): Forms on grey: painted by Paule Vézelay when she was living in Paris. Oil on canvas, 1935*

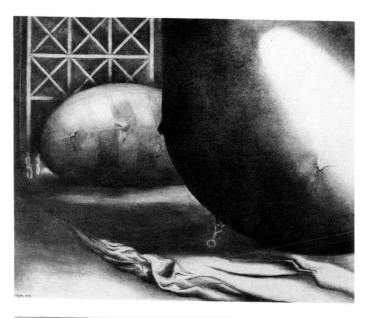

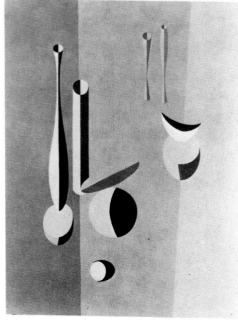

10 & 11 *Dora Russell (above) with Bel Mooney in her garden, 1983, (below) aged 18*

12 *Sydney Street, 1923. A candidate and his supporters. In the foreground, left to right, Stella Browne, Dora Russell, Bertrand Russell*

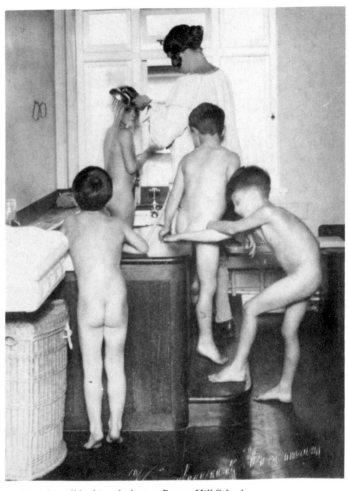

13 *Dora Russell bathing the boys at Beacon Hill School*

14 *Dame Flora Robson at home in Brighton, 1983*

15 *Flora Robson in the play which made her an overnight success:* The
Anatomist *by James Bridie, 1932*

16 *As Queen Elizabeth in* Fire Over England, *1936*

17 & 18 *Dame Janet Vaughan (above) at home in Oxford, 1984, (left) aged 23*

19 & 20 *Opposite (above) Blood donors: a temporary clinic set up in a factory, 1944, (below) Janet Vaughan gives her blood*

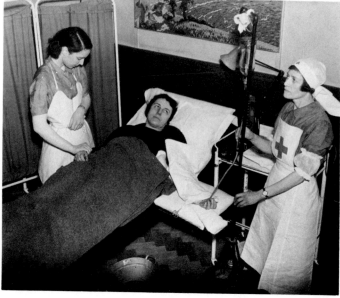

21 *Portrait in oils of Janet Vaughan as Principal of Somerville College.
Painted by Claude Rogers, 1957*

22 & 23 *(above) Baroness Wootton at home in Abinger, 1983, (below) as a young girl*

24 *Baroness Wootton on the day she took the oath at the House of Lords. She was one of the first life peers in 1958*

insisted on being friends with all the "baggage" behind the iron curtain. All the Labour people who went to the 1952 Peace Congress in Vienna were kicked out of the Party.'

Dora involved herself especially with women's peace activities, travelling in 1951 to the Soviet Union with a women's delegation, then in 1955 helping to set up the Permanent International Committee of Mothers, which sent a delegation against war to the United Nations. In 1958 she created the Women's Caravan for Peace, which travelled throughout the whole of Europe, East and West. The precursors of CND, she says, were a small group of women meeting in a Hampstead coffee-house. In 1957 they organised a women's march at which women like Edith Summerskill and Joyce Butler spoke.

'At that stage I was on the original committee, and I wanted them to carry on as they were, without seeking a lot of influential support, because I thought it should involve lots of ordinary people.' But then CND came into being, and one of the influential figures roped in was of course Bertrand Russell. 'I didn't feel that I should be involved in it now, given my separation from him, so I had to become, so to speak, a rank-and-file member. I took part in all the Aldermaston marches, sleeping on church-hall floors and so on, but I was never a committee member again.'

This parallels her decision, twenty years earlier, not to write about Beacon Hill School, since Bertrand Russell was writing hostile articles about the subject himself, and she didn't want to become involved in a public controversy with him. In effect, she subsided into obscurity for the sake of keeping their personal problems out of the issues she cared about.

It was not until Bertrand Russell had died, in 1970, that Dora was able to set about putting the record straight with her own autobiography. Although out of the public eye for many years, she had not ceased to be active, in any way she could, for the things she believed in. Often it was a case of the causes themselves failing to get any attention. Dora cites the example of the National Union of Teachers' conference in 1960 on 'Popular Culture and Personal Responsibility', which warned that the mass media were having a harmful effect on the moral and cultural standards of young people.

She has also watched the progressive industrialisation of China since Chairman Mao's death with increasing concern, as, she thinks, would he. 'Like some of us in the West, he had seen Russian political ideals defeated by the power of the industrial machine. He was trying a new way – decentralising, combining industry and agriculture communally, marrying the intellectual and peasant cadres. Given the Chinese philosophical background and temperament, the plan had some chance of success, which it will now never have the opportunity to prove. The devouring juggernaut grinds on its way.'

It's hard to imagine Dora Russell being in anything but a minority, at least for the foreseeable future. Few people have so tenaciously (and from so early on) opposed the Great Machine of the twentieth century. She seems to me, for all her anti-religious attitudes, and her faith in human progress (in the sense of feeling we *can* make good rather than bad use of science and technology), to be first and foremost an opponent of materialism. This showed all too clearly in her early distaste for the United States, and was reiterated in a passionate letter she wrote to her mother in 1921, whilst still in China with Bertrand Russell: 'I am filled with hatred for money, for battleships, for industry, for factories, for the grind, grind, grind of the machine on all our creative instincts, grinding out the good and putting power in the hands of evil. Comfort is brought at too high a price. Let us scrap industry, even if we go ragged and hungry, and lift our hands and square our shoulders and say at least we are men now, not cogs in a diabolical machine of destruction.'

And indeed, this destructiveness has touched her very personally, for her youngest child, Roderick, was crippled for life in a mining accident at the age of twenty-three. Always a supporter of his mother's ideals, he preferred to do his years of military service amongst miners than in an army which proposed to use nuclear weapons. It was he who encouraged Dora to persist with *The Religion of the Machine Age*, which she was at last able to show to him just before he died in 1983.

Given the dark moments she has faced during her life, Dora Russell's spirit is remarkably undimmed. She is strong-minded, argumentative, opinionated. Once she gets going, it's hard to get a word in edgeways. But she is also warm and generous, with an unflagging enthusiasm for life in all its variety. She believes that women hold the key for the survival of this life, and that this is their greatest, and indispensable, strength. Not that she sentimentalises her sex's capacity for nurturance (her satire on Rousseau in *Hypatia* makes that clear enough). She simply wishes that what is abused and taken for granted and trivialised could be seen as what it truly is: the powerful force that keeps the world from flying apart.

It would be easy enough to shake one's head and decide that her life only shows how trying to turn prevailing forces on their heads is an enterprise doomed to failure. Granted, her ideals have not been realised in such a way as to instantaneously prove their worth. But to portray her in this way is to assume that her life is a self-contained unit, to be assessed (by some computer, perhaps?) according to the quantity of goals achieved or not achieved within a set span of time.

For me to do this, I would have to ignore one of the principal lessons of her life, which is that human history is full of surprises. It unfolds in an organic, not a mechanistic manner. Seeds scattered at one point in time, whilst appearing to die, spring up from the earth when you least expect them. The pain of birth does not constitute failure. Her capacity for surviving adversity, and still returning to assert her faith in herself and her kind, is to me an object lesson in patience.

Besides, as a woman, I acknowledge the space that the unashamed upheavals of Dora Russell's life have made for the rest of us. She too, in *Hypatia*, paid jubilant homage to the feminists who preceded her.

'We, who in a sense are the children of the feminist pioneers, whose thoughts embrace the universe, whose lives are one long round of mental and physical delight, at time intense to ecstasy – we at least will pay our tribute to those who lit the sacred fires, before we take up pen and paper to criticize.'

It is surely time that her words be offered back to her in turn.

Flora Robson

Flora Robson was born in South Shields in 1902 but was brought up in the London area. She studied at the Royal Academy of Dramatic Art, and made her first fully professional stage appearance in 1921. She worked in various provincial theatres before receiving critical acclaim in 1931 for her performance in James Bridie's *The Anatomist*. Some years at the Old Vic theatre followed, and from the 1930s until her retirement in 1970 she starred in a great number of plays and films. She was awarded the DBE in 1960. Two biographies are: *Flora Robson* by Janet Dunbar (1960) and *Flora* by Kenneth Barrow (1981). Dame Flora Robson was interviewed for the television series by Joanna Lumley.

'I want to act in all the little villages. I haven't much longing for the West End.' (1943)

'An actress must feel a lot. The more you mix with the public, the more you learn to feel.' (1983)

Flora Robson

Dame Flora Robson took both my hands in hers and, exclaiming that they were like blocks of ice, drew me to the fire and offered me a drink. This was the cosy sitting-room I had seen through the windows as I walked along the terrace of Victorian Gothic houses in Brighton, where Dame Flora has lived for the last nine years or so. Before that she had lived in another part of Brighton, but had moved here with two of her sisters when one of them was widowed.

In the gathering darkness of a frosty winter afternoon, that room, with its quaint Gothic windows, elegant furniture and pleasantly subdued lighting, could almost have been a set from one of Dame Flora's plays or films. Young writer arrives to try and recapture a living legend of the British stage . . . Her down-to-earth friendliness, however, prohibits fantasy and keeps any encounter with her firmly on a level of simple human exchange.

Before coming to visit Dame Flora Robson, I had felt myself to be at something of a disadvantage, in that my memories of her as an actress stem largely from old films viewed on sleepy Sunday-afternoon television, or in archive material sometimes shown of her on the same medium. I had never seen her on stage, and indeed was only fourteen when she retired from the theatre in 1970. The strongest association Dame Flora evoked in my mind was Queen Elizabeth I, both in *Fire Over England* and *The Sea Hawk* (films in which she had marked my Sunday-afternoon senses more forcibly than most actresses of her generation), and, incongruously, in a hilarious sketch on the Morecambe and Wise Show.

But whether used in earnest or in fun, her slightly husky voice, with its blend of sensuality and perfectly modulated English, has, I am sure, entered even my modern consciousness and given me some sense of what it means to be an Englishwoman, with all the strange dignity, the powerful, yet paradoxically restrained, passion of that condition. Her great gift, it seems to me, is to have played her roles in such a way that ordinary people could to some degree empathise with them. Whether they were seeing the 'frustrated spinster', the 'villainess' or the 'royal personage', what mattered to Flora Robson's audiences is that she made them believe in the person within the shell, the human essence beyond the social type.

Although she is called the uncrowned Queen of Brighton by the locals, she is not in the slightest sense imposing. In fact the title is more a reflection of the love she elicits in those around her, than a symbol of some abstract status she might have amongst them. Her house is constantly full of people, both family and visitors. She takes a direct and warm-hearted interest in adult and child alike. Though the widowed sister is now in a Home, another sister remains to share her everyday life. When I visited her, I was surrounded by a mêlée of dogs and their owners. Flora likes dogs almost as much as she likes human beings.

She gave me the same undivided attention she gives everyone else, and yet she struck me as being extremely sensitive to everything going on around her. When the windowpane rattled, she said, 'Oh it's only the wind,' and when a visiting dog barked in the next room, she paused in what she was saying to wonder briefly which dog it was.

As we chatted and sipped our drinks by the fire in her sitting-room, I gained some impression of the presence Dame Flora Robson must have carried with her on stage. She has never been conventionally beautiful, but this very fact has given her face an enduring quality that even now, in her early eighties, remains. In actual fact, nothing could be more beautiful than the very strength of her features: the wide, full curve of her lips and the large, deep-blue eyes that seem to drink in everything around her. And though she has lost two inches off her original height of five foot nine, she still stands with the erectness and moves with all the graceful assurance of the trained performer. Like her hand-clasp, everything about her is firm and direct, though gentle.

In this atmosphere of relaxed warmth, it seemed natural to talk first about her family, which was for Flora the emotional foundation on which her career rested. She was the sixth of seven children, five girls and two boys, born to Eliza McKenzie, a sea-captain's daughter who had married David Robson, her father's second engineer. Both of them had moved from their native Scotland to South Shields, where David Robson worked as a marine surveyor in a Tyneside shipbuilding firm. This is where, on 28 March 1902, Flora Robson was born. Since she was born on a Good Friday, her godmother said that all her sins would be forgiven.

Certainly the family was a happy and close one. Flora, however, received less attention from her mother than she might otherwise have done, since the brother who was born two years before her was a sickly child and required a lot of care from Eliza Robson. But this lack was made up for by a specially close relationship with her father, who used to take her on his lap and teach her poems, once giving her a shilling because she learned so quickly to recite them back to him. She was also close to her mother's brother John.

'He was only fourteen when I was born, but when they used to push me out in my pram and leave me alone to look out at the green fields opposite, he would come and talk to me. We became great friends. When he was ordained around the age of forty, I used to take him on holiday sometimes, since he couldn't afford it on a vicar's salary . . . I found out that it was him who pressed my father to let me train properly for the theatre.'

By the time she was five, after several moves, her family had settled in Palmers Green in London, where she attended a small school. This school was run by a woman who had nursed ambitions to be an actress.

'But she was the thirteenth child of a lawyer and they'd never been able to afford any training for her. Anyhow, she put on this school performance in which I was supposed to recite "Little Orphant Annie". I was only five at the time, and they carried me on stage and told me to wait for the curtain to go up and then begin reciting. I had on these new white socks of which I was very proud, and everyone laughed because I had bent down to pull them up just as the curtain rose. Anyhow, after my recitation, I went to find my father who was talking to the teacher, and he turned around and said excitedly, "You're going to be an actress!" And she said, "You're going to be my private pupil!" And I thought, oh dear, this means I'll have to stay in after school again. And that's what it's always meant. When other people are going out and having a nice time, I've always been going to work.'

And so, while the other children were going out to play, Flora often had to stay in for lessons in singing, ballet, piano – or, most importantly, elocution. With all the attention going to her brother or her youngest sister, the baby of the family, she badly wanted to please her parents, and she worked hard. Her father took her to see her first play, *Faust*, at His Majesty's Theatre. 'The only thing I can remember about it now is that the leading lady started to strip at one stage, and I was shocked – would she ever stop? I can't remember how far she got!' Her father already thought of her as 'our next Ellen Terry', and enthusiastically encouraged her to appear in concerts and recitals. Her fame spread so she was soon being asked to appear in places like the Lyceum Ladies' Club in Piccadilly. One of her star turns was the tragic story of 'The Little Match Girl'. William Stewart, Professor of Elocution at Hampstead Conservatoire, trained her voice and entered her, at the age of ten, for the Royal Academy of Music examinations in verse-speaking, where she collected the bronze medal – the youngest ever recipient of this award. She also won second prize at the British Empire Shakespeare Society competition.

As a child performer, she wasn't simply sweet or ingenuous. A musician engaged by her school to teach the class to sing once made each child repeat a certain line individually. 'He came to me and I sang the line and he looked at the headmistress and said: "She's got a *voice*!" That was all, but I'll never forget it.'

When she turned thirteen, however, she began to suffer from a kind of stage-fright, and her glands swelled every time she had to perform. So, for several years, she turned away from the theatre and simply attended Palmers Green High School with her sisters, doing well in her studies. Getting a distinction in the Junior Oxford exams led her to try for the Senior Cambridge, but she was held back by a weakness in algebra and geometry, and she failed to get a scholarship to Cambridge. 'So I thought right – acting!'

She went to study at the Royal Academy of Dramatic Art, having persuaded her father that she was definitely serious about her ambition and that it was worth him stretching his meagre financial resources to support her training. He didn't, of course, disapprove of his daughter becoming an actress for moral reasons, as many people at that time would have done. David Robson had a decidedly romantic feeling for the theatre. In many ways, Flora has dedicated her career to this father who was always her most appreciative and loving audience.

At RADA she not only took acting classes, but also learned to fence, to fall and to move properly, and continued to do ballet and vocal training. 'I was quite well ahead because my voice had already been so well trained.' A term after she arrived in 1919, Kenneth Barnes, having just returned from the war, took over as

Principal of the Academy. He was to become a good friend, trying to help her find work in the difficult early days of her career. Another teacher who had a great deal of influence on her was the Scots actor Moffat Johnson, whom she describes as another father-figure, and with whom she continued to correspond for many years after he left for America at the time of her graduation. While Flora was at the Academy, several distinguished figures visited to give classes, including Sir Gerald du Maurier and Sybil Thorndike, who, along with Helen Haye, taught Flora the virtue of holding back her emotions for the climax of the scene.

By the end of her course, Flora Robson was in line to win the coveted Gold Medal which would have helped her entry into the professional theatre and even a job in the West End. But a few days before the public show on the grounds of which the awards would be given, she came down with the flu and nearly lost her voice. As a consequence, she only won the Bronze Medal.

Now she had to make her way up the slippery slope of professional acting. Though her voice, her ability to learn parts quickly and her intelligent, hard-working attitude to her craft were to stand her in good stead in the future, they were not what agents and producers were looking for in the short term. For Flora did not have the pretty, *ingénue* look which was needed to win so many youthful parts for women.

'I was always ever so old, even at seventeen, and yet they didn't want to give me older parts, either. When you're young but not pretty, they just don't want you. And there weren't any good parts for women. They wanted young women to back up the men, that's all.'

After Kenneth Barnes had given her one more chance to show what she could do in a Sunday-night performance of *Undercurrents*, a play he wrote himself, she did finally manage to get her first fully-fledged professional part in Clemence Dane's *Will Shakespeare*, which opened on 17 November 1921 at the Shaftesbury Theatre. As well as her own small part (the apparition of Queen Margaret), she also understudied several others, and when the flu epidemic which swept Britain that year was at its height amongst the cast (this time leaving her unaffected), she found herself playing three parts in one night.

By this time her family, on whom she was so dependent for emotional support, had moved out of London to Sussex, and Flora hated living alone in London digs. She felt very insecure and nearly gave up the theatre altogether; however, she knew she had to earn her own living, and acting was after all what she had trained to do. So she managed to get herself engaged for six months in Ben Greet's touring Shakespeare Company, starting in Bristol in March 1922. This experience was not much happier than the first one. Another actress in the company was jealous of Flora, and did everything she could to make her life difficult, including disrupting her performance. Greet was not a supportive presence either, once shouting to Flora in the middle of a performance that her shoes were all wrong (she hadn't been able to afford to buy any others and the company did not provide footwear).

Her next engagement was with J. B. Fagan's and Jane Ellis's repertory company based at the newly-created Oxford Playhouse, which opened, after some initial opposition from the University (the vice-chancellor thought there were enough distractions in the town as it was), in October 1923. Flora played Nurse Guinness in a revival of Shaw's *Heartbreak House*; Shaw himself was in the audience. She was also in her first production of *The Importance of Being Earnest*, as well as getting her first solo curtain call in *The Return of the Prodigal* by St John Hankin.

Whilst at the Oxford Playhouse, she met Tony Guthrie (later known as Tyrone Guthrie), who like herself was one of the youngest actors in the company. Both of them were unfortunately dropped after two terms, precisely, says Flora, because their youth limited the parts they could play. This left her once more high and dry, looking for work with little chance of success, since no London managers had ventured as far as Oxford and she was still completely unknown. Eventually, things got to the point where she would have to take any kind of paid work she could get, even outside the theatre.

'My sister Lila, who had lost her fiancé during the war, was living at home and helping out there. She said to me, "If you don't get a job, I'll have to," and I didn't want that. My father had already spent a lot of money on me, and I wouldn't live off him any longer. So I went to work as liaison officer at the Shredded Wheat factory in Welwyn Garden City where my family were living at that time. Of course then my father was furious and went around saying, "I've spent all this money on her and then she just goes and works in a factory!" But I'll never run down my time in that factory, because I learned a lot about people while I was there, and this was invaluable for my work later on.'

During her four years at the factory, she acted as a kind of receptionist, taking visitors round and directing people to the right department. She also acted as a welfare officer, listening to the workers' problems and taking them to the management.

'Most of the work was done on one floor, but there was one man cooking the wheat in two big cylinders upstairs, all on his own. Once I noticed him looking a bit pale and ill, and I asked him what the matter was. "Well, I'm left up here feeling as though I were left out of everything," he said. So I went to the management and told them, and they sent in another man for a week, and they changed places every week after that.'

She was less successful in helping the women who were employed as packers in the factory. When the management wanted to speed up production, they would pay the men a penny an hour more. But the women got nothing.

'The speeding up of the machines meant that the girls had to work very much harder packing the biscuits into boxes,' she told her biographer, Kenneth Barrow. 'The girl at the end was never able to catch up as she was all the time pushing the unpacked product to one side. Whenever I had an hour to spare, I used to go down and help them pack. The management did not like this, nor were they sympathetic when I pleaded the girls' case over the speeding up. I was accused of spoiling them, of taking the heart out of them. I said it wasn't a very good advertisement taking visitors round the factory, seeing sweat pouring down the girls' backs.'

Flora Robson hadn't during this time given up the desire to go on stage – far from it. She would store up the impressions and emotions of the day, then go for long walks at night and think about the theatre. 'I was like a champagne bottle, absolutely longing and bursting to act.'

Meanwhile she was able to direct some amateur productions with the workers at the factory in a small theatre they built – the only theatre at that time in Welwyn Garden City. 'I directed a thriller, and a children's play on Saturdays. They would go home from the factory and dress in their best clothes, then come back with their girl-friends or boy-friends and sit in the audience until it was their turn to go on.'

In order to design her lighting plots, Flora used a book written by the lighting director of the Cambridge Festival Theatre. This was one of the most exciting experimental theatres going – far more so than Fagan's theatre in Oxford, and she nursed a secret longing to work there. Early in 1929, she needed a judge for an amateur drama competition in her area, and she asked Tyrone

Guthrie, who had branched out into producing for radio and writing drama. She enjoyed seeing him again, and showing him her theatre.

'I pointed out a set and said, "Isn't it lovely? It reminds me of the Festival Theatre in Cambridge." He looked at me surprised and said, "Do you want to go back into the theatre?" I said, "Oh! I'd give my eyesight to go back!" He said, "Well, I'm going to be Director at the Festival Theatre in Cambridge." Bang on! Just what I wanted! He sent for me in London and around March I auditioned. They accepted me but said they didn't start until the autumn. So I did another six months in the factory, saved my money up very carefully and had a holiday, then went back and said, "I'm going to leave in a fortnight, I'm going back to the theatre." And I've never looked back since.'

The time at the Festival Theatre, says Flora Robson, was one of the happiest phases of her career. At last she was used to full advantage, first in Pirandello's *Six Characters in Search of an Author*, and then in a succession of interesting roles in plays which included *Iphigenia in Tauris*, where she played opposite Robert Donat as Orestes, *Measure for Measure*, *Lady Audley's Secret*, *The Cherry Orchard* and Pirandello's *Naked*, in which her performance was hailed as 'flawless'. She was supremely happy to be working with Tony Guthrie, whom she describes as her 'guiding angel' and even as her Svengali. He had been one of the first people to recognise her special gift for performing with an emotional integrity which rarely failed to sweep the audience up into empathising with even the most unsympathetic or alien characters.

During this period, Guthrie asked her to marry him. But there was a fundamental difference between them: she wanted children, and he did not. Flora's view of marriage was drawn from her own family's example of domestic warmth and closeness. The relationship hung fire for several years before Guthrie finally married his cousin Judy Bretherton instead. Flora never really thought seriously of marriage again, concentrating instead on her career. 'Right after the Great War, when my older sister Lila had lost her fiancé, I remember being told I was one of four million surplus women, and thinking, right, I'll marry my job.'

Indeed, she may have fed this home-loving aspect of herself directly into her work. Many of her colleagues have witnessed not only to the brilliance of her acting, but also to the kindness she showed them, both on and off-stage. It was almost as if she made the theatre, wherever possible, a home from home, transposing the values of her own family into the dressing-rooms and the wings. One of the aspects of theatrical life she enjoyed most, she says now, is the company spirit that pervaded places like the Festival Theatre. And her favourite audience of all time was that University audience, who formed a loyal and appreciative following for her long before she became famous.

There was one occasion, when she was walking along the tow-path by the river, learning her lines, when the man in the bow of one of the rowing eights noticed her. 'He tapped number two on the shoulder, number two tapped number three, and so on, until they had all recognised me and were madly waving away at me! The other people on the bank couldn't think what was going on . . .' On the first night of the Leonid Andreyev play *Betrayal*, which had transferred to London and thus brought Flora's Cambridge days to a close, the entire Pembroke College Boat Club turned up to toast her in her dressing-room afterwards.

Cambridge had marked a real turning point in Flora Robson's life. For the first time, her seriousness as an actress had been used to the full, under Guthrie's perceptive direction. Indeed her devotion to her work and her ability to learn lines quickly may even have been a little overtaxed. Late one night the stage manager found her at the back of the theatre, frantically rehearsing her lines for yet another part in her tight schedule. 'He sent me to bed and told Tony he really ought to put off the opening night or I would collapse. Tony agreed.' Her hard work, at any rate, had now paid off, and she was ready to move on to greater things.

Flora's appearance in *Betrayal* at the Little Theatre in London was what first attracted the notice of the influential *Sunday Times* critic James Agate to her work. Agate was to be a staunch, though not uncritical, ally over the next period of her career. After this, she appeared in Eugene O'Neill's *Desire under the Elms*, which had been banned by the Lord Chamberlain and could only be shown at a private club theatre – in this case the Gate, under the arches at Charing Cross. It was now that she met Sybil Thorndike once more. Dame Sybil had been persuaded to come and see the play by her son Christopher Casson, and afterwards she went backstage to congratulate Flora, and to ask her where she had learned to act. She had forgotten that she herself had once taught her, and even provided letters of introduction for her.

'I thought, my goodness, here's a new sort of face in the theatre,' recalled Dame Sybil later. She remarked to her husband Lewis Casson that this was 'a tragedienne who's going to be as big as Edith Evans is in comedy'. Dame Sybil was, says Flora, the first person to make her feel really welcome in London, and she generously tried to put Flora in contact with other people who could further her career. It was at this time in 1931 that Flora made her film début, in *Dance Pretty Lady*, directed by Anthony Asquith, in studios which were situated, conveniently enough, at Welwyn. As she cycled to work, all her old friends from the factory would wave at her.

Anmer Hall, who had managed the Cambridge Theatre, then gave her a contract in his newly opened Westminster Theatre at Victoria. The first play was *The Anatomist* by James Bridie. Flora was thrilled to be directed once more by Tony Guthrie, and to be playing with the then famous Henry Ainley, whom she had admired for so long. Once, as she came off-stage from rehearsing her part as the Scottish prostitute Mary Paterson, sobbing for pity of a young doctor whose heart had been broken, and now falling unwittingly into the power of the body-snatchers Burke and Hare, Ainley was standing in the wings. '*You* know how to do it,' he said to Flora.

Ainley was right. After the first night, there could be no more doubt that Flora Robson had arrived. Ten years after her first stage appearance, she was hailed as an actress of the first order. Agate called her performance 'an exquisite piece of acting'. St John Ervine wrote: 'If you are not moved by this performance then you are immovable and have no right to be on this earth. Hell is your place.' The critic from *The Times* wrote: 'She brings out with the most delicate skill the tenderness which may be latent in the depths of degradation, and carries off all the honours.' And James Bridie himself recorded later that Flora Robson 'gave a performance of such appalling beauty that she burst the play in two'.

Yet even though she was such a success, Flora continued to suffer from a crisis of self-confidence, both about her looks, and about her future. She had a habit of expecting the worst, even when things were going well – perhaps *especially* when things were going well. Emotionally, she was in many ways very vulnerable, and this affected her entire view of the world. She began to feel doom-laden and insecure about what she would do after this high point was over. And then, as she told her biographer Kenneth Barrow, she suddenly realised how she was hurting herself by falling prey to these feelings of inadequacy.

'I remembered the positive thinking that had taken me to Cambridge and the happy glorious time I had there. There was no reason why my entire future should not be the same. What a fool I had been. Here I was, a successful actress in a hit play. Why should it not be the beginning of a brilliant career? I decided I must make the best of what life had brought me and believe in myself a little bit more.'

A brief revival of Pirandello's *Six Characters* helped her to do just this. The *Daily Telegraph* critic, W. A. Darlington, called her 'an actress with a genuine emotional gift, whose future should be worth watching'. Then came an opportunity to play the pivotal role of Olwen Peel in J. B. Priestley's *Dangerous Corner*, which, before opening at the Lyric, Hammersmith, was tried out in Glasgow. Flora had expected to feel at home in Scotland, since her parents had come from there and all her ancestors were Scottish, but to her surprise she was treated as a 'Sassenach'. She felt, she says, as though she had no real country to call her own.

Though it got a mixed reception from the critics, *Dangerous Corner* was a commercial success. Flora got on very well with Priestley, who has described her as 'one of those exceptional actresses who could dominate a scene without . . . hard edges, maintaining a deeply feminine quality'.

The only problem was that she might begin to be typecast as a 'hysterical spinster', an impression which was confirmed by her appearance in Somerset Maugham's *For Services Rendered*, after which Priestley wrote to her that she would be well advised not to take another part of this kind. Flora was indeed in danger of having her talent for conveying emotional intensity trap her into playing one neurotic character after another. Yet the part of the deranged Ella Downey in O'Neill's *All God's Chillun Got Wings*, where she played opposite Paul Robeson, was a logical outlet for her talents, nonetheless.

Robeson was subsequently to become a lifelong friend. 'He used to come down and visit my family in Hove, and call my parents "Mum" and "Dad". He also used to tell my father all the nice things people were saying about me.'

Flora in turn told Robeson's wife Essie that she didn't think black actors should meet racial prejudice with humility, but rather with dignity, especially when playing a role like Othello. 'You cannot hurt people who have dignity.'

In 1933, Flora Robson played the part of the Empress

Elizabeth of Russia in *The Rise of Catherine the Great*, made by Alexander Korda's company, London Films. It wasn't a tremendous success, but in the meantime she had achieved a long-term ambition by getting a contract with the Old Vic company, along with the newly successful Charles Laughton. 'He was always very nice to me: he told me that in films, since you couldn't project as you do in the theatre, you should make your face into a pudding – relax the chin – then when you think of something it comes through your face.'

On stage, however, Laughton was not so easy to get on with. He would play to the audience, whereas Flora had been trained on the Stanislavsky principles, and expected a movement of give and take between one actor and another on the stage. But she loved the Old Vic. 'We all wanted to play there, not only because of the Shakespeare, but also because of that loyal audience. They followed you wherever you went, and cheered the place down! You really felt you were *loved*.'

Whilst at the Old Vic, Flora made her mark in both comedy and in tragedy, with *The Importance of Being Earnest* and *Macbeth*. She has, however, never been terribly happy playing comedy. 'Tragedy has been my stuff. I don't think I have a sense of humour!' Nonetheless, she was still able to make audiences fall about with laughter, if only because of the incongruous solemnity she brought to many of her comic roles. Her Lady Macbeth, on the other hand, was something of a controversial performance.

'I saw her as an unimaginative woman. She pushes her husband to the limit, and then doesn't want it to go any further. Unimaginative people are horrified by the results of what they do. "'Tis safer to be that which we destroy, than by destruction dwell in doubtful joy," she says. In the sleep-walking scene, I made it clear she was asleep, and not mad.'

But for many of the critics, and for James Bridie who wrote advising Flora to 'stop being psychological', this interpretation was not convincing. Some thought that Lady Macbeth should not be portrayed in so sympathetic and down-to-earth a manner. Alone of his colleagues, Darlington gave her a rave review: 'If there has been a finer Lady Macbeth in our time I have not seen her. She had all the baneful horror of a Medusa, and yet managed to show a pitiful humanity.'

Flora decided that she was not, after all, happy playing Shakespeare. 'He never wrote terribly good parts for women.' James Bridie, on the other hand, did write such parts. And in spite of his response to her Lady Macbeth, he had written a play especially for Flora. This was *Mary Read*, drawn from the true story of a woman pirate. She used her holiday on the Scilly Isles with her eldest brother and the rest of her family, as well as tales of her sea-going forebears, to prepare for this role. The fencing lessons she had taken all those years back at RADA also came in useful.

Flora was a great success in this colourful role, playing opposite Robert Donat, with whom she had always got on well. The London opening was at His Majesty's Theatre, where she had seen her first play, *Faust*, so many years ago. 'Her dash and zest and dare-devilry, and faith and courage, and ringing voice, and – at the right time – feminine tenderness and sacrifice, roused the audience to such a pitch of enthusiasm at the finish that the rest of the company forgot all about themselves and just joined in – one of the rarest of all tributes,' wrote one critic.

By this time, Flora was under contract to Korda's London Films, who wanted to have her play Queen Elizabeth I in *Fire Over England*. This was a role she had hankered after for years, having read a great deal about this, her favourite monarch.

'I must have lured the part to me because I already knew all about her. During her reign, the whole of Europe was having religious wars, but she steered England down the middle of all that. "Take away those candles," she'd say, "it's not dark." I think she was the beginning of our conservative attitudes.'

The contract meant Flora could draw a regular salary (Korda even sent her away on holiday to Egypt at one point), but the film was a long time in preparation. In the meantime, she took a couple of additional theatrical roles, one of which required her to play opposite the Austrian actor Gustav Homolka, a relationship which was in marked contrast to the sympathetic and cooperative one she'd enjoyed with Robert Donat.

'It was a play with only two characters and he wouldn't act with me. I had to put my arms around him, and he'd been wearing the same shirt for weeks. I think he did it on purpose. But he's dead, so I don't mind saying these awful things about him. He was the only actor who ever really acted *against* me.'

She also played a short run as Mary Tudor in Wilfrid Grantham's play of the same name. It was at this time that she wrote to a friend about the relationship between her personal feelings and her work.

'My own sorrows get mixed up with the play, especially the longing for a son. I can always identify with that. Sometimes I feel the part intensely, usually the performances after matinées. The more tired one is, the more one's emotions rise to the surface. But my technique is improving so much that I can act sorrows well enough to convince myself, and that brings up the real feeling again. There is hardly a single night when I have not cried in the last scene.'

When, in the spring of 1936, filming finally began on *Fire Over England*, Flora found that her role as Mary's succesor was not as interesting as she had hoped. The film was built around a young woman Korda was grooming for stardon, Vivien Leigh. She played a lady-in-waiting with whom Laurence Olivier (as Leicester) was in love. Flora's part was cut to a minimum. However, she soon showed what she was made of, shooting one pivotal scene in a day and saving the company thousands of pounds. Then she suggested she read Elizabeth's original speech at Tilbury, rather than the truncated version that had been written for the film. 'I know I have the body of a weak and feeble woman, but I have the heart and stomach of a king, and of a king of England too . . .'

This caused something of a sensation. The speech was not as well known then as it is now. 'Pure Churchill stuff, of course,' says Flora. This was the Robson role that caught the imagination of audiences all over the world. 'The one quality which stands out above any other in Flora's performance,' wrote Kenneth Barrow, 'is her warmth, a rare commodity in the cinema of the thirties.'

Her next role was to have been as the Empress Livia in Josef von Sternberg's *I Claudius*. But this ill-fated project was never completed, and she turned her attention to a much more low-key role in a film called *Farewell Again*. Korda had been against her doing this, as he now conceived of her as a 'grande dame' of the screen. But her performance, which gave her another opportunity to display the emotional sensitivity of her acting, was well received by public and critics alike.

The next phase of Flora Robson's career took her back to the theatre, where she played in Ibsen's *The Lady from the Sea* and O'Neill's *Anna Christie*. In 1937, she scored one of her greatest triumphs, in Margaret Kennedy's adaptation of the Russian playwright Ilya Surguchev's play, now titled *Autumn*. She played the part of a barrister's wife who falls in love with a younger man, only to see him gradually turn his attention to her stepdaughter. When the play opened in Manchester, before coming to London, the *Manchester Despatch* critic described Flora's performance as the greatest acting he had ever seen, and gave a telling description of her unique appeal.

'Her face, with its attractive rugged contours, is so marvellously expressive. Darkly sullen when she is brooding, it lights with a sudden radiance into strange beauty when she smiles.'

When the play opened in London, W. A. Darlington confessed that he sniffed all the way back to Fleet Street. Flora's Uncle John, who as usual was in the audience with her father, told her that in the interval, one man was so overcome by emotion that, when he tried to light another man's cigarette, his hand shook to the point where he nearly ignited his friend's beard! Flora was also summoned to see Queen Mary in her box and be congratulated on this play and on *Fire Over England*. On tour with *Autumn*, Flora was greeted with just as much enthusiasm wherever she went. In Blackpool, a woman in the audience sobbed loudly all the way through Flora's own crying on-stage.

Although she won that year's *Film Weekly* award for best actress, Flora's contract with Korda was not renewed. It seemed that she did not have the glamour to make her into what he thought of as good box-office material. She began to feel more than ever that her tombstone would eventually bear the words 'She was a plain woman'. However, all was not lost, for in 1939 she was taken out to Hollywood to play the housekeeper in *Wuthering Heights*.

There she earned the respect of William Wyler, who was directing, and seeing her once make a face at something, he asked her to advise him. This was an English classic, he said, and he wanted it to be liked in England. At the end of the filming, it was suddenly decided to put in the voice of the housekeeper as narrator throughout the film. Since most of the writers (including the young John Huston) had left by this stage, Flora wrote her own lines for this, keeping as close to the original novel as she could.

The danger now was that she would be type-cast as an eternal housekeeper. It was for this reason that, after returning to England to make *Poison Pen*, she turned down Alfred Hitchcock's offer to play Mrs Danvers in *Rebecca*. But Warner Brothers offered her two other films in Hollywood, *We Are Not Alone*, with Paul Muni, and *The Sea Hawk*. In the latter, she was once more to play Queen Elizabeth, this time opposite Errol Flynn.

'People are always surprised that I liked Errol Flynn – none of the other actresses did. I realised that it was probably because he was brought up in the theatre; he liked playing opposite me, because I didn't simply act to the camera. He didn't like the fact that other actresses didn't act to *him*. Errol and I got on like a house on fire. There was a scene in which Elizabeth was meant to come out and stop a fight between two of her men, and Errol persuaded me, as a joke, to say "break it up, boys, break it up". The director, Mike Curtiz, was terribly upset, but I didn't let on whose idea it was . . .'

Immediately after this, Flora made her Broadway début in *Ladies in Retirement*. By this time, the war was making it impossible for her to return to England: it was too dangerous to cross the Atlantic. She ended up stranded in the United States for four years. Though she was very homesick, and worried about her friends and family in England, she made the best of her time in America. During a seven-month tour of *Ladies in Retirement*, she learned a lot about ordinary American people, frequently speaking to groups like Women's Institutes in the afternoon, before appearing on-stage in the evening.

She was beginning to enjoy her public persona, and the warmth with which she responded to her admirers only re-inforced her popularity all the more. She was a rare kind of actress – one without pretensions or arrogance. She had taken to heart the lesson Moffat Johnson had taught her at RADA: 'If you succeed, do not think you are a special person. You are no better than a good workman plumber. Learn humility.'

She realised that she enjoyed bringing her work to the varied audiences who came to see her on tour just as much, if not more, than playing to the sophisticated playgoers of London or New York. Towards the end of her time in the United States she told John Van Druten, who with Lloyd Morris had written a play – *The Damask Cheek* – especially for her, that she didn't want to transfer with it to London. 'Over Christmas when I heard carols I burst into tears and became very homesick. If I go back next year I shall go to the Old Vic. I want to act in all the little villages. I haven't much longing for the West End.'

One of these small engagements took the company perform-ing *The Damask Cheek* to the army base at Fort Meade. Flora enjoyed the rapturous reception there, but declined to dine in the officers' mess when she discovered that the black woman who was her maid was not to be included. She had another, and stranger, brush with colour prejudice when she took the part of a mulatto woman in *Saratoga Trunk*, and was harassed as she made her way, in full make-up, to the set. 'It really brought home to me what it's like to be coloured,' she says.

In 1943, she was finally able to cross the Atlantic, having been given priority in order to return for a tour sponsored by the Council for the Encouragement of Music and the Arts. The tour, which took her, as she had wished, all over Britain, was an adaptation of Emile Zola's *Thérèse Raquin*, entitled *Guilty* and directed by Tony Guthrie. Sadly, he and Flora no longer got on as well as they once had, and this was more or less the last time they worked together. England in the war was a bleak place, compared with the United States. When Flora appeared as the slave Ftata Teeta in the film of Shaw's *Caesar and Cleopatra* in 1944, there was never enough hot water for her to remove the heavy body make-up properly.

In 1945, just before the London opening of *A Man about the House* which brought her back to the West End after a seven-year absence, her father died. This was a great blow to her, since she had always felt his appreciation of her work as a constant factor throughout the ups and downs of her career. Now he was no longer there in the audience. The person to whom each new triumph was an offering of love had gone. Four years later, she remembers, when appearing in *Black Chiffon* on the West End stage once more, she was feeling this loss particularly keenly.

'I couldn't get into the right *mood* for the play. I was standing in the wings, thinking how much I missed my father and wishing he were out there to watch me. Then all of a sudden the curtains were caught in a breeze, and lifted up, and I thought, "He's here!" Then we took the play to America, and again I was looking at the curtains, but they were quite still and I thought, "Oh dear, he hasn't come." But just at that moment a hurricane hit the theatre and the curtains went *whoosh*! I was so pleased!'

In the late forties, she also discovered that she could do a tremendous amount for charitable causes by making radio appeals, such as the one which in 1947 raised five thousand pounds to help the Skolt Lapps of Northern Lapland, whose livelihood had been destroyed during the war. For this, Flora was awarded the Finnish Order of the Lion and the White Rose for Services to Humanity, and was told when she received it: 'In Finland, you are regarded as second only to God.'

In fact it had been as a result of her brilliant portrayal of a nun in the film *Black Narcissus* that she had been asked to make the appeal in the first place. Flora's faith has always been, along with her family, the thing that sustains her in her work and influences the way she relates to other people. She always prayed before going on stage, she says.

'I have a saying: ask God's blessing on your work, but don't ask him to do it for you. But I always ask the Holy Spirit to inspire me – I say, "I've done everything I can, now please come and be with me as I go out there." I know that my acting, you see, is a gift from God . . .'

Yet after the successes of productions like *Message for Margaret* in 1946, and a revival of her role as Lady Macbeth with Michael Redgrave, which they took to Canada and the USA in 1947, Flora's gift did not get as many chances as it should have done to shine, either on stage or on screen. The fifties were a patchy decade for her, in spite of a few good parts such as Paulina in a production of *The Winter's Tale*, directed by Peter Brook for the Festival of Britain in 1951. This performance is said to have been one of the first truly modern renditions of Shakespeare. Brook was later to write to Kenneth Barrow, agreeing with this verdict. 'With Flora, the down-to-earth understanding was coupled with the extraordinary warmth and intensity of her personality.'

During her late forties and early fifties, she was not offered many parts that were up to the standard she had set herself before the war. However, she did reach a larger audience by appearing on television in plays like *The Corn is Green* or as nurse Edith Cavell in . . . *And Humanity*. The television medium suited her well, and she was one of the first of the classic British actresses to make such good use of it. When her colleague Sylvia Coleridge confessed to Flora that the early television cameras seemed like advancing brontosauruses to her, Flora advised her to 'take three deep breaths and feed them with nuts'! She also continued, of course, to work in that peculiarly stable medium – radio. By 1958, she had over 120 radio credits to her name. She was also awarded an honorary degree by Durham University.

Then, in 1959, the sparkle was restored to her career, when she took the role of Miss Tina in Michael Redgrave's stage adaptation of *The Aspern Papers* by Henry James. Here at last was a part that stretched her to the full once more. It is probably for this role that she is, in modern theatre, best remembered. A. Alvarez wrote that Flora's intelligence and skill matched Henry James's as the creator of her character. She won the *Evening Standard*'s award for Best Actress of the Year – the first time she had been officially rewarded for her work in the medium she most loved – the theatre.

In 1960, Flora was sitting in her dressing-room when her dresser brought her a letter. On opening it, she burst into tears.

It did not bring news of some tragedy: it simply told her that she had been created a Dame of the British Empire (she had already received a CBE in 1952). Yet she felt that all those who had been truly close to her, and would most have appreciated the honour, were gone: for both her mother and her Uncle John had died within a few years of her father.

This last decade before her retirement in 1970 was mostly taken up with film work. She disliked much modern theatre of the 'kitchen sink' variety, and, in the other direction, the antipathy of a critic like Kenneth Tynan to her style of acting didn't help her career at this point. On the other hand, the Newcastle repertory theatre named 'The Flora Robson Playhouse' in her honour. She played the Empress Tzu Hsi in Nicholas Ray's *Fifty-five Days at Peking*, in which some irresponsible dyeing of her hair made it fall out. Undaunted by yet another set-back to her looks, she went on to make films like *Murder at the Gallop*, the delightful *Young Cassidy* and *Seven Women* (which was the last film John Ford ever made). 1966 was what she called her 'Greek year', since she made the Anglo-Greek film *A Cry in the Wind* and then played Hecuba in Sartre's version of *The Trojan Women*. The following year the BBC devoted an entire season of plays to her with a 'Flora Robson Festival'.

In 1967, however, Dame Flora triumphed on the stage once more – in a comic, not a tragic, role this time – as Miss Prism in her one-but-last production of *The Importance of Being Earnest*. One critic said this performance would 'fix the role for future generations as Edith Evans once fixed Lady Bracknell.' Then, after a couple more stage productions (*Ring Round the Moon* and *The Old Ladies*), Flora Robson went into official retirement.

I said that the 1967 performance was the one-but-last *Importance of Being Earnest*. This is because, retired or not, she could still on occasion be lured out, as she was when her old friend John Counsell at the Windsor Theatre asked her to play in Wilde's classic one last time. She also made quite a few more television appearances, in all-star productions like *The Canterville Ghost*, *A Man Called Intrepid* or *Les Misérables*. In 1980 she played in *A Tale of Two Cities*, in which her solemn way of playing comedy paid off beautifully once more. When as Miss Prosser she confronted Madame Defarge (played by Billie Whitelaw) and declared with high dignity: 'I am an Englishwoman,' everyone watching fell about with laughter. She was equally stupendous in *Alice in Wonderland*, in which the 'off with her head' song is quite unforgettable, and in her last appearance as

Miss Fothergill in L. P. Hartley's *The Shrimp and the Anemone*.

The fact is that Dame Flora Robson can never entirely retire, even if she no longer appears on stage or screen. She is too much a part of British culture to be allowed to retreat into obscurity. In 1974 even Oxford University acknowledged this by giving her an honorary degree (soon after she had participated in the Golden Gala of the Oxford Playhouse, whose boards she had been one of the first to tread fifty years earlier). She is constantly called upon by charities and by local groups such as the Youth Orchestra, of whom she is a much-loved patroness.

'I go and sit in the audience to support them,' she says, 'and do you know, they suddenly call out my name and flowers are handed over the footlights to me! It should be the other way round, really. And they always play Elgar's *Nimrod Variations* for me when I go.' She pauses to sing a few bars. 'In the early days, music was my second love after acting. I played the piano very well and used to accompany my sister Margaret who played the violin. I still love music – but not jazz or pop. I love to sing in Church – remembering to *breathe* properly! Second only to music is silence. I love silence. These days I go to bed early, just to be alone and quiet, to read the Bible or think about the day . . .'

The value of stillness has shown itself throughout Dame Flora's acting career as much as in her personal life. She has had the gift of generating tremendous power in a *seemingly* effortless manner. She once compared this with less disciplined acting by using the images of a Rolls-Royce and a taxi. 'One is making an awful lot of effort and not getting anywhere, the other has everything going *inside*, smoothly oiled and running, and getting there very quietly.'

If she has not always had the chance to make the best use of this gift at every point of her career, it is nonetheless acknowledged and remembered by anyone who has seen her in her element, as Sir Laurence Olivier's eloquent tribute to her makes clear: 'The whole festival of talents that has always been in Flora caught one in an always surprised, utterly real way. The combination of her voice, looks, personality and sheer acting genius, once seen, haunts one for ever.'

Janet Vaughan

Janet Vaughan, born in 1899, had an ambition to become a doctor. She studied at Somerville College, Oxford, and University College Hospital, London, qualifying in 1924. Her career was mainly in research; she specialised in diseases of the blood, writing papers and books on that subject. In 1939 she set up one of the first blood transfusion depots. She became Principal of Somerville College in 1945 and was a member of several government committees. She was awarded the OBE in 1944 and DBE in 1957. Dame Janet Vaughan was interviewed for the television series by Polly Toynbee.

> *'Always throughout my working life there have been these two, sometimes conflicting, forces: the desire to help redress the ills of society, and the desire to help push forward the frontiers of scientific knowledge.'*
>
> Janet Vaughan

As I approached Dame Janet Vaughan's house in Wolvercote, North Oxford, I could see her through the large picture window of her living-room. She was sitting at a round dining-table, with numerous papers spread out in front of her. 'I don't sit around knitting, you know,' she had said, a little sharply, when I rang a few days earlier to ask if we could change the time of our appointment. And so I crunched over the gravel to the front door of the modern, mellow Oxford brick-built house with the inevitable feeling of slight trepidation that comes from knowing you are about to interrupt someone in mid-concentration.

The figure that greeted my ring, however, was warmly welcoming. 'Sorry I barked at you on the phone,' she said, 'it's been a bad week. I'm trying to get a paper on radiation cataracts ready for publication. There it is, you see,' she added, showing me into the large front room in which I had glimpsed her earlier.

She had the house built when she retired as Principal of Somerville College in 1967, and the proportions of this room, she said, were taken from a room in the Principal's house in which she had felt particularly comfortable. She liked the light, too, from the south-facing windows giving on to her garden. Evidence of her gardening instincts were visible inside the room as well, with a healthy collection of plants overlooking the table currently devoted to radiation cataracts, including a large dazzling red lily. At the other end of the room were a comfortable collection of chairs and a sofa, amongst which she invited me to sit down. On a low table were a collection of books, mostly autobiographies, which Dame Janet explained are her favourite form of light reading. This and walking, at least in the days before arthritis struck in earnest, have always been her principal ways of relaxing. One gets the impression that time off from work has never included anything which didn't in some way stretch either mind or body.

Janet Vaughan is a handsome woman. Observing the silver-grey hair swept up behind her head, the long face and nose, the rich dark eyes with their slightly languid look, I wondered if the knowledge that she is related to Virginia Woolf was interfering with my perception of her, or whether there was indeed some distinct family resemblance here. In spite of the leg-brace, necessitated by her worsening arthritis, she insisted on moving about the room, showing me things or getting us tea. The apparent ease and speed of her movements belies her age, as do her upright posture and the casual dignity she exudes, even despite her jumper and comfortable slacks.

As we sat near the bookcase lined with tome after tome of 'my dear Bloomsburies', she watched me avidly consuming the delicious cakes she had made that morning and told me I'd come on the right day. She's not the domesticated type, she says, but on Wednesdays she cooks lunch for an old friend normally catered for by meals on wheels, and so she bakes something for tea too. There's nothing half-hearted about Dame Janet Vaughan: when she does something, she does it properly. Throughout my conversation with her, two of the qualities that most struck me were her humour and her pride. Not pride in herself, really, but in her work, which she has always found, and continues to find, utterly absorbing.

She still goes to the library every day and tries to keep up with the ever-increasing volume of literature in her field (blood and bone disorders and the physiological effects of different radio-active isotopes), and she still attends seminars. 'It's nice to hear them answering questions I raised in the 1930s,' she says. 'Just the other day, they were all in a frightful twitch of excitement, having got hold of two cases of a very, very rare bone-disease. When they started looking at the literature, they found that I had done the post-mortem on the first one in 1932!'

Medicine, says Janet Vaughan, is in her blood. Her great-great-uncle on her father's side was Henry Halford, physician to George III, George IV, William IV and Queen Victoria, and President of the Royal College of Physicians. And he was only one in a long line of family members who were drawn to medicine as a career. On her mother's side, her great-grandfather, John Addington Symonds, was also a physician and a member of a traditionally medical family.

Janet Vaughan's father, William Wyamar Vaughan, was not a doctor, however, but a teacher. When Janet was born in 1899, he was assistant master at Clifton College, after which he became Headmaster of Giggleswick grammar school in the West Riding of Yorkshire, and then Head of Wellington College and of Rugby. He was, she says, a fairly radical man when it came to matters of education, though he was also deeply conventional, and disapproved of his wife's literary and artistic friends and everything to do with what became known as 'Bloomsbury'.

Janet was much closer to her mother, a beautiful, amusing and brilliant woman whom she describes as 'a caged bird'. Unable to make a serious contribution to the life of the schools where her husband worked (he disapproved of involving a headmaster's family in the school), she was nonetheless, after her marriage, cut off from the life she had loved as a girl. She had been the constant companion of her father, John Addington Symonds, living with him in the Swiss Alps and Venice, and sharing his friends and interests. One of these friends was Leslie Stephen, father of Virginia Woolf, to whom Margaret Symonds was very close as a girl, until her marriage to William Vaughan drove them apart. Woolf later drew her portrait as Sally Seaton in *Mrs Dalloway*. It was, however, through the Stephens that Janet Vaughan's parents first met, since William Vaughan was Virginia's cousin. In her (as yet unpublished) memoirs, Dame Janet describes an incident which characterises the tension between her parents, and her mother's personality.

'She retained the innocence of her strict Victorian upbringing, and once described to me her despair when my father had found some book by Symonds [i.e. her father] and Havelock Ellis – I now presume *Sexual Inversion*, and burnt it in the grate of his Rugby study. "I don't know what all the fuss was about – Greek love or something," she said to me, a rather bewildered adolescent.'

When her younger sister Barbara died, Janet became the only girl in the family. Her two younger brothers were sent away to school, but she was taught mostly by a governess, before being sent at fifteen to North Foreland Lodge, which at the time was supposed to be one of the best schools for 'young ladies'. It was 1914, the start of the First World War, and the school was evacuated to Great Malvern, where Janet promptly caught pneumonia and nearly died. 'My chief memories of the war, both at home and at school, are of cold and never-satisfied hunger.'

Her favourite subject was history; she had a keen interest in current affairs as well as the issues of poverty and social justice. She decided that in order to be in a position where she could do anything about these things, the best thing she could become was a doctor. But when she was seventeen, her headmistress, who didn't take this ambition seriously, told her father that she was 'clearly too stupid to be worth educating'. She thought his daughter should be encouraged to take up social work in the East End instead.

Certainly, she derived very little benefit from her school

career. When she came to apply to Oxford, she had to take the entrance examinations three times before she got in. 'First I failed in every single subject, then I passed in Latin Grammar and Arithmetic, and then my mother brought me up for the third time and we stayed at the Mitre and had a lot to drink – and for some reason I got through! I still wonder if they didn't mix my papers up with someone else's . . .'

The only science she had done at school was 'a little ladylike botany'. Now she had to catch up in physics and chemistry. 'I was a public danger, because there I was in the lab handling phosphorus and acids and things, and I knew nothing about them at all. I think my fellow students kept a rather safe distance from me at first. But I ploughed through the necessary subjects in the end.'

At this time, just after the war, there were only a handful of women studying medicine at Oxford. Janet Vaughan studied at Somerville College, which one of her aunts had helped to found, though it was not as yet accepted by the University on the same footing as the men's colleges. During the summer vacation at the end of her first year, she was sent off by her prospective tutor, Dr H. C. Basett, to read through the whole of a classic textbook on physiology.

'The discovery of the world of knowledge that opened up for me, reading physiology as expounded by E. H. Starling, was the beginning of an adventure that has gone on for me ever since. I began to think less that summer of reforming the world and its ways, and more of just the excitement of learning how biological mechanisms explained biological observations.'

Not that she gave up her extracurricular interests altogether. She became the only woman member of the Mazzini Society, which used to meet in New College for the purpose of discussing modern political affairs. In order to attend the meetings, she had to be chaperoned by Miss Jebb, a Somerville don. She also became president of the college debating society, and chaired the famous row between Vera Brittain and Winifred Holtby, of which she says: 'Vera took the line that we were all children, as indeed we were, compared to her with her experience in the war as a VAD. Finally, after twenty-four hours of extreme tension I managed to persuade the two of them to make up their differences and thus began their great friendship.'

While at Oxford, Janet made friends with a number of different people, including medical contemporaries such as Sybil Eastwood and Cicely Williams (who during the Second World

War was interned in some of the worst Japanese POW camps). She also made friends with Robert Graves and his family. 'I can't remember how I got to know Robert, but he lived in a cottage out at Islip. I used to go out there and see him and Nancy and the children, and talk about books and life and all that. Robert always used to make mugs of tea which he brought round to us in bed in the mornings . . .'

She got to know the Huxleys and the Haldanes. Margaret Huxley was in the same year as her at Somerville, and it was through her that Janet received a message that Jack Haldane would be prepared to teach her. Her tutor at Somerville, Miss Kirkaldy, did not approve of this, since in her opinion Janet's interests were already far too wide-ranging, and 'JBS would distract me further from the strict syllabus'. But Janet held firm, and went off every week, complete with chaperon, to New College.

'This of course was a piece of unique good fortune. Jack Haldane had a superb mind, one of the great scientific minds of his generation. In the 1920s he was interested not only in classical physiology, but also in rapidly expanding subjects like genetics and psychological developments in neurology . . . He encouraged me to read widely and write critical essays, though admittedly he often went to sleep when I read them aloud to him! This wide reading perhaps accounts for the "maid-of-all-work" sort of science I have always enjoyed, piecing together knowledge from many different disciplines to make a somewhat simple whole.'

The stimulation of tutors like Haldane and Basett turned her around, academically, and in her physiology finals she pulled off a first-class degree. 'My family were of course very surprised. They thought I was just jogging along, and here all of a sudden the daughter who wasn't worth educating had won through!'

That summer she and her mother, who was immensely proud of her ('it sort of vindicated everything'), went on holiday together in Italy, where she developed an enduring appreciation for good paintings and the Italian countryside. She describes her mother as having 'a great capacity for always making every ordinary thing exciting'. Then she returned to Oxford for two terms to study pathology and pharmacology, before embarking on her clinical experience at University College Hospital in London, for which she had won a Goldsmith's scholarship. Once again she was thrown in the deep end.

'The first night I was put on to casualty there was a staff

shortage, and a woman came in with her face split open. The casualty officer simply said "sew it up" and walked away. I hadn't a clue as to whether to use a straight needle or a curved needle, catgut or silk thread. Fortunately there was a very tactful sister there who handed me the right instruments and I suppose I sewed the face up fairly successfully.'

Her consulting surgeon used to throw scalpels at his students if patients in the operating theatre were not properly prepared, 'but he taught us well'. She then did her medical clerking to the children's physician, Frederick John Poynton, who specialised in rheumatic fever. 'I can see them now – sometimes six or seven children at a time propped up in bed with rheumatic hearts, often with pericarditis as well as endocarditis. This is something the welfare state has almost banished from the English scene. How anyone could do medicine in those days and not become a socialist I find hard to understand! It was so obvious that so much illness and suffering was due to poverty. What I hated most was the people's acceptance: "Yes, I have had seven children and buried six, it was God's will." I hated God's will with a burning hatred.'

Her first experience of midwifery confirmed these feelings. 'I went out with another student to see her deliver a baby, then as soon as I came back I had to take out another student and show him how to do it. I had never seen a proper delivery. During the war, when one had to turn one's hand to almost anything, I was always frightened I might have to do a proper delivery. . . . But of course I learned a lot of other things, because we worked up behind Euston, where there was terrible, terrible poverty, women giving birth with nothing but newspapers to lie on. At night we rode bicycles, and sometimes if we asked a policeman the way he would say: "Oh I wouldn't go there, miss, it's pretty rough," but go we did – that was our job. One night I climbed a dark rickety stair to be greeted by a very belligerent husband: "Ain't there any men doctors? We'd rather have a black man than you." However we parted good friends. The old half-tipsy attendant promised to come and rub my back when my turn came. I learned no obstetrics that month, but much of human courage and endurance and the love of men and women.'

She qualified in the summer of 1924 'in spite of spelling vomiting with two ts' (her spelling had been consistently bad all through her academic career – in fact she now attributes her illegible handwriting to 'self-protection'). After this she spent her last holiday with her mother, who was to die in 1925. This death was not only shattering in personal terms, but turned out to have professional repercussions too.

'It was at once clear that I must give up all idea of becoming either a consultant physician or a general practitioner as I had wished and planned,' she later wrote in her autobiography. 'To become either I should need to take several resident hospital appointments, but it was obvious that I must be free to come home at least for weekends, and if necessary for one or more nights in the week, to look after my father and to entertain for him in the School House at Rugby.'

Although this was a tremendous wrench for her, she tried to make the best of it. After a six-month house job at the South London Hospital for Women, she became an assistant clinical pathologist at University College Hospital. Luckily, her superior, C. W. Goodhart, believed in connecting clinical medicine with pathology, and so she was able to get to know all the patients whose specimens she examined in the laboratory. In fact throughout her career, she has, one way or another, succeeded in doing some clinical work alongside her pathology and her research. One of the first areas she became interested in was blood diseases.

'Having been trained at Oxford, I had continued to read all the literature, and I saw that in America they were treating pernicious anaemia – from which you could die at that time – with whole liver. Now this story is a measure of how medical research has changed. I went, a little junior clinical pathologist, to the Professor of Medicine and showed him how well people I had fed with liver had done. I said I wanted to try to make some extract of liver as they had done in America. He gave me some money and told me to go and buy some liver and make some extract myself. So I went and borrowed all my friends' mincing machines and pails – the sort of thing they used to scrub floors with you know – and sat up all night with the book beside me and started to extract my liver. I knew no chemistry really, and the description in the literature was very inadequate, but finally I had made a jam jar full.

'I took it to my Professor and asked if I could give it to a patient on the ward. "Oh no," he said, "we must test it on a dog." So it was tested on two dogs and they both were sick. By now I had very little left, and I was determined no more was going to be wasted on dogs, so I said I'd take it myself. The next morning, when I came back to the hospital after taking it, the Professor and two of his colleagues were waiting on the doorstep to receive me. I looked very well; so then I was allowed to give it to a patient, who in fact was a great friend, he was an old labourer, you know, and he took the extract and it worked. He recovered.'

One of the people Janet borrowed a mincing machine and a pail from was Virginia Woolf, who lived just near her in Bloomsbury. She also used to leave her bicycle in the Woolfs' hall, since she couldn't keep it at her digs.

'She was very kind to me when I came to London, always interested in what I was doing, asking me about cycling around and what it was *like* riding up Piccadilly – she was always fascinated by facts and information. I was very useful because in the General Strike I could run errands to important newspapers and so forth – I think there's an account in a memoir which says "Here was Janet with her bicycle who could go". She was very beautiful and full of fun, and her marriage with Leonard was a very secure one, the sort of marriage it's always good to find.'

Janet met her own future husband, David Gourlay, in the digs in Taviton Street, which was actually a communal house, run by a group of men and women who had worked together in the War Victims' relief organisation in France. Gourlay, who had been a conscientious objector in the First World War, was a founder member of the house, and ran the Wayfarers Travel Agency with his friend Geoffrey Franklin. 'Their idea was to enable and encourage people of different countries to meet and get to know one another and so to reduce the inevitability of war in the future.'

She also knew many other Bloomsbury figures, including Clive and Vanessa Bell, and befriended artists like the Russian sculptor Dora Gordine, for whom she and David Gourlay managed to arrange a prestigious London exhibition. The delightfully earthy figurine of a laughing woman that Gordine gave them in thanks still sits on Dame Janet's mantelpiece today. Her father did not approve of her Bloomsbury associations, even though some of them were his own relations. He said at one point that he washed his hands of his daughter. Her brothers, too, were much more conservative than her, though she never argued with them overtly. 'The fact that I achieved some success, in spite of my odd ways, was a constant surprise to them.'

Yet Janet liked the Bloomsbury group for what she describes as their 'integrity'. 'They lived according to their beliefs and without regard to the world and its criticism. They were men and women of great intellectual ability who cared passionately about their different disciplines. They were in no sense dilettante . . . Bloomsbury never bothered to rebel, they just lived their own lives assuming that all moral questions must be scrutinised in the light of reason . . . and that the most valuable states of mind are those associated with the contemplation of beauty, love and truth.'

It was in the light of Bloomsbury that she had come to understand the homosexuality of her own grandfather, John Addington Symonds, and when she discovered that much of his work on sexual inversion had been destroyed by Edmund Gosse and Hagburg Wright (the librarian of the London Library), she was very angry. 'What right had those two old men to destroy the work of another scholar for their own moral satisfaction? . . . Living in Bloomsbury I accepted that the loves of men and women were their own affair, and that as long as harm was not done to others, moral problems did not arise.'

In 1929, William Vaughan remarried, and Janet was free to fully take up her own life once more. She went to the United States on a Rockefeller Travelling Fellowship, to study under George Minot in the Thorndike Laboratory in Boston, where the work on pernicious anaemia she had read about had originated. Minot, who later won the Nobel Prize for his discovery of the cure for this previously incurable condition, became a firm friend and corresponded regularly with Janet until his death. 'He was one of the great physicians in the tradition of Harvey, Jenner and Addison, whose work was the starting point for a sudden leap forward in our understanding of disease.'

After her months in the USA, during which she was also sent on a tour of laboratories and hospitals in other parts of the country, she returned home to marry David Gourlay. 'David and I had talked much of our plans before I went to the States. I was to go on working and, for my work, I would keep my maiden name, not for any feminist reasons, but because I had already published several papers, and it seemed a pity to lose my medical identity. It was fun, too, for me to be two people. When we went on holiday and were around together, I was Mrs David Gourlay.'

After a short spell at a large non-teaching hospital in London, she went as a Beit scholar to the London Hospital, working on the connection between blood and bone diseases under Professor H. M. Turnbull and Donald Hunter. Though they, along with the neuropathologist Dorothy Russell, were very welcoming, the other members of the staff were not so friendly towards women physicians. 'Dorothy Russell and I always had our meals with the secretaries, and if anyone wanted me to see a patient, they would write me a note – would I be kind enough to go and see Miss Smith in ward six. Then I'd write a note back saying what I'd found, and never a word was spoken apart from this.'

She also worked on blood disease cases in Donald Hunter's outpatient clinic in the East End of London, where she realised more clearly than ever the effect that poverty had on health. Many of the women she treated with iron for anaemia would ask her to stop because the medicine made them hungry – and they couldn't afford the food.

She became part of an ad-hoc committee which produced a bulletin on malnutrition, publicising the work of people like Helen McKay who proved that anaemias in infancy were due to a lack of iron – something which was not yet acknowledged. This work came to an end with the outbreak of the Second World War, but Dame Janet feels it played 'perhaps a small part in formulating ideas enshrined in the Beveridge Report. It certainly strengthened the belief that some of us had in the importance of "social medicine".'

She feels that much of this disease was eliminated, ironically, through wartime work and rationing. 'Everyone was drafted, you see, and that meant they ate in canteens, largely. And so they got adequate – I don't say luxurious – but adequate food. The poor ate far better than they'd ever eaten before. For the rich, of course, it wasn't so pleasant.'

When she gave birth to her first daughter in 1933, she had just finished her first textbook: naturally enough, it was on anaemia. This child was followed two years later by a second daughter. The babies spent a lot of time in their prams (under cat-nets of course) in the garden of Gordon Square when the Gourlays lived in a flat above the Wayfarers' office. Their upstairs neighbours were Charles Laughton and his wife Elsa Lanchester, and Janet remembers Laughton's nerves before playing Macbeth opposite Flora Robson at the Old Vic. Bloomsbury, she says, was full of psychologists and psychiatrists, and one day, as she pushed the eldest child, Mary, out in her pram, she was approached by James Strachey, who was working on the Freud papers, and who told her that she shouldn't have given the child a rattle.

'I smiled a little anxiously and pushed the pram a little further, to meet Adrian Stephen, a practising psychiatrist. "Oh Janet," he said, "I'm so delighted to see you've given the child a rattle. That will help to ensure a stable personality in later life." I felt a great relief, and decided that I had better perhaps depend on common sense rather than theories.'

By 1934 she was working at the post-graduate school at Hammersmith Hospital, where other members of staff, to her relief, *did* condescend to greet her when they passed her in the corridor. This was a happy time in her life. She had a live-in nurse/housekeeper to look after the children while she pursued the work which absorbed her (the back of the car, she says, was always 'full of interesting specimens'). And she loved living in Gordon Square.

'The garden had several different populations. In our day there were many young children who, as soon as they heard the Wall's bell on hot summer afternoons, would set off on two legs or four, depending on their age, towards the ice-cream man. Later in the evening would come small groups, Roger Fry, Clive Bell, Leonard and Virginia Woolf and Julian Bell to sit and talk and talk as darkness fell.'

Her experience of social conditions, and the rise of Fascism in Europe, led her to become increasingly involved in politics. As well as linking poverty with malnutrition and working in the birth-control campaign (in the same clinic, at one point, as that which Naomi Mitchison was involved in), she also threw herself wholeheartedly into the Committee for Spanish Medical Aid. The Spanish Civil War was, she says, the political event that had the most effect on her life. At one point she even joined the Communist Party, since the Labour Party 'somehow seemed so feeble' in the face of the issues which concerned her, and she was impressed with the 'determination and personal quality' of party members whom she had encountered. Not liking to be led, ideologically, she soon lapsed, however, though her brief membership originally caused her problems getting a visa to the United States.

The week before Munich, the post-graduate medical school was told in confidence to be prepared for up to 37,000 casualties in London that weekend. This was, as it turned out, a little premature, but it did galvanise Janet and her colleagues into setting up crude transfusion sets and collecting blood for storage, a technique that was still fairly new, medically speaking. It was said afterwards that 'the only blood shed at Munich was what Janet collected at Hammersmith'.

'Having got all this blood I thought we'd better find out how to use it, because the future didn't look terribly secure. So with another very good physician, Guy Elliott, I started using this blood on hospital patients. It worked like magic, and Guy delivered a paper on the subject to the Royal Society of Medicine. Some of us who were concerned about transfusion in London got together in my flat in Gordon Square and discussed the sort of arrangements we ought to have for blood storage and transfusion in case of war, how to collect donors, what sort of bottles to store it in, how to transport it, and we wrote a memorandum – a group of utterly self-appointed people – about providing London with blood. We thought there should be four depots, one at Slough, one somewhere down in Kent, and so on.

'Anyhow we sent this document off, out of the blue, to one of the men we knew was responsible for planning emergency services. My professor then came along to see me one day and said: "You're a very naughty girl, Janet. What are you doing sending all these memoranda around?" I just shrugged my shoulders and said we'd had a few ideas and thought we'd better put them down. Finally the authorities came back to us and said they wanted the thing costed. I went and consulted my friend the Dean who had been a very senior army doctor, and he said we should treble all our costs. Then we were given official instructions to go to our respective towns and set up blood-donor centres.'

Having sent the children off with their nurse to the supposed safety of the Gourlays' cottage near Guildford (though in the event more bombs fell there than on Slough), David went off to a civil service job in Glasgow and Janet went to Slough. There, the chairman of the trading estate helped set her up in the social centre, next to the bar, with space outside for special refrigeration units. Being next to the bar proved important when it came to finding donors and drivers in an emergency! Refrigerated vans were requisitioned from Wall's to transport the blood.

'Three days before war started, I got a telegram from the Medical Research Council which said: "Start Bleeding." That Sunday we stood in the social centre bar in our white coats with the locals, to hear Chamberlain state we were at war, and then we went back to our bleeding.'

She had a group of doctors and qualified scientists on her team, but the rest of the staff of VAD nurses, secretaries, technicians and drivers were drawn from the immediate vicinity. 'Two local girls were trained to make all the sterile plasma and serum, and sterile they kept it in spite of the really unsuitable dusty conditions in which they had to work. I always remember Dr Bourdillon, a high-powered expert sent down by the Medical Research Council to advise us, looking regretfully through the glass windows of the "sterile room" and asking me if I could not persuade the girls to put paraffin on their hair as well as on the floor and tables to keep down the dust. I pointed out that at least they were wearing caps. Paraffin might not have been good for morale.'

As the war progressed, the Slough unit acquired a reputation for reliability and efficiency. As soon as they saw the bombs begin to fall on London, they would be out with the vans and on their way. 'It soon became known that if there was a disaster anywhere in England, you rang up Slough. So when Liverpool was hit and their blood transfusion service was absolutely kaput, they called us in. I went into the bar and asked if anyone would drive up there with all the equipment, and of course I got someone straight away. Being next to the bar had another advantage which shouldn't be despised in a crisis – we could always get some whisky! That was very important to the young girls who had been driving through terrible weather and blackout.'

Under the extreme wartime conditions, there was no way that Janet was going to be confined to the role of pathologist. She was soon confronted with the numerous civilian casualties of the blitz. At one point during the war, she attended a meeting of the Medical Research Council to discuss what was happening with these casualties. As the only woman, she was the first to be asked to relate her experience of treating shock amongst the wounded. 'This was extremely alarming, because I was a pathologist, and in my experience the casualties had not at all fitted the classical picture of shock. Basically, I had found the wounded had high blood pressures and not low blood pressures as we had been taught to expect.' Having ventured, in some trepidation, to say this, she was relieved to hear it confirmed by several young clinical doctors.

This resulted in a new understanding of wound shock, which stood the medical services in good stead when it came to Dunkirk. It was at this point that, having run out of blood, they started using plasma instead – still a very experimental thing to do, since they were not sure the plasma they had stored was entirely safe. This, says Janet Vaughan, is one of the advantages of doing medicine in a war: if you don't try something a bit risky, people are going to die anyway, and so a great many medical advances and discoveries were made, arising out of sheer necessity. Quite often, desperate measures turned out to have seemingly miraculous results.

'I shall always remember one night when we went up to an

incident on the Great West Road. There was a little girl who was so badly burned there were no veins left. I put her on one side – in those days you just took the people you could save – and we set up the transfusions with the VADs on the people we thought had some hope of survival. Then I went back to the little girl, and having read that you could sometimes put blood into the bones, I took the largest needle I had in my pack, and stuck it into her sternum, attached a bottle, and told the VAD to keep pumping while I went to attend to another crisis somewhere. When I got back two hours later, the VAD said she'd got in two pints. Well, we got in three pints in the end, and the little girl lived and went off and had skin grafts. Later, when I was at Somerville, a head-mistress wrote and said I might remember one of the girls coming up from her school, because I'd transfused her in the war, and there she was with her little claw-like hands. So we took a good deal of trouble with her, though someone said she might not be good enough academically. I said I'd saved her life once, I would take her in now. And she did well in every way.'

The emergency medical services had scattered many doctors who previously had only worked in the Greater London area to other parts of the country, and there was a growing realisation amongst members of the Royal College of Physicians that medical services would have to be improved and brought up to the same standard all over Britain. As a Fellow of the Royal College, Janet used to attend their 'Comitia' meetings.

'I shall never forget the time when all the old gentlemen were talking about the future of medicine, the future of surgery and so forth, and without thinking I jumped up and said: "Well, what about social medicine?" – then sat down, plomp, again. Afterwards, several old gentlemen came up to me and said: "My dear, no woman has ever spoken in Comitia before." No younger fellow had ever spoken before, either, but afterwards a committee was formed and we wrote a great memorandum about the necessity for crèches and all the other things that constitute social medicine.'

In 1944, she once more found herself the statutory woman (a role she confesses she has always rather enjoyed), this time on the Goodenough Committee, which looked at the post-war organisation of medical education. The heads of all the medical schools were asked to answer three questions. Would they accept academic professors with charge of academic departments in clinical subjects? At this point most teaching hospitals used Harley Street consultants and did without academic departments of their own. The second question was: would they accept medical students from the Commonwealth, irrespective of race? And the third question was: would they accept women? The answer to the first two was a grudging 'yes' (in the second case because 'they owed it to the Empire').

'Then we came to "would you accept women?" I sat there very demurely, and one or two of them actually said that under no conditions would they accept women! However, it was finally made a condition of receiving a government grant that they should accept women.'

After this Janet, once again the only woman, was sent to India by the government together with Professor Ryle and an official of the Ministry of Health to give evidence to the Bhore committee, then sitting in Delhi, reviewing medical education and services. The great historian of medicine, Henry Sigerist from America, and a representative from Australia were also in the party. The Russians failed to arrive. Cannily, Janet asked for some clothing coupons so that she could take the appropriate cotton dresses for the heat – and even, to her great delight, a glamorous evening dress for formal occasions. 'It did much for my morale as I walked down great staircases in Government House, though it sometimes aroused surprise, as expressed by the viceroy's private secretary one evening at a grand party. He couldn't understand why anyone as smart as me in my silver lamé frock could be trailing round India looking at bore-hole latrines.' Her male companions, she recalled in her memoirs, were often too exhausted to go sight-seeing as well as doing their work. Not so Dr Vaughan: she set off alone to see everything from the Sphinx (they travelled through Egypt on their way to India) to the Taj Mahal. Her father had met his death there by falling off the legendary palace whilst on a visit with the British Association, and she was able to visit his grave.

Whilst she was relieved to get away from the bombs and the grimness of life in wartime Europe, she was struck all the more forcibly by the impact of poverty, far worse in India than at home, on the health of the great majority of people. In her memoirs, she relates her feelings during a return to the University of Karachi a few years later.

'As we drove out through the terrible slums – miles of hovels made of sacking and old bits of corrugated iron, with no sanitation, no lighting, no water – to the university, I wondered whether higher education for a few could ever meet the desperate needs of the many.'

After her return home, she found herself involved with research into starvation – in this case amongst soldiers and civilians in Europe who had come out of the prison camps. A new treatment of giving them concentrated protein in liquid form – called protein hydrolysate was being tried out. Shortly before the end of the war, she was in the offices of the Medical Research Council when some medical officers came in and said they needed someone to go to Belgium and treat cases there.

'The MRC said: "Well, here's Janet, she's good at sticking in needles," so I was put into uniform that night and sent off the next day with two others. One was the distinguished chemist Rosalind Pitt-Rivers, the other a young physician, later Professor Charles Dent. I made the rounds of the hospital in Brussels and said I didn't think there was much starvation here, so they said they'd uncovered a concentration camp at Belsen and would we go there? I said yes, if they didn't tell the Medical Research Council, because we hadn't had our typhus inoculations.

'So they gave us a lorry and told us to "liberate" any equipment we might need, and we set off the next morning on the back of an open lorry with our precious hydrolysates. But they couldn't spare us an armed guard, because they were short of men. We drove over the Rhine on wooden bridges, and everyone was terribly excited to see two women on the back of the lorry.'

Belsen was only twenty miles from the front. She saw forced labourers of many nationalities streaming out of camps in their striped pyjamas (as a consequence, when she got home she burned her husband's striped pyjamas). They knew when they were getting close to Belsen by the smell of faeces and dead bodies. The only medical personnel there consisted of a single field ambulance. When the Captain in charge of it greeted Janet and her colleagues with relief at the thought that they'd come to help, she was forced to tell him that they were really only there to see if the protein hydrolysates would work.

'His face fell, but he was magnificent and gave me a room and two Hungarian soldiers to assist in chopping up the furniture to burn in the stoves and move the patients in so I could try treating them with the hydrolysates. The trouble was, it was nauseating stuff and I had nothing to make it taste good. I remember one day I found a few onions – frightful excitement all round! But when I tried to give them the hydrolysate intravenously, they would shriek: "Nicht crematorium! Nicht crematorium!" You see the Germans had injected them with paraffin so that they would burn better . . .'

She battled on through the nightmarish conditions, realising that the hydrolysate treatment was not proving effective, at least under these conditions; once again she was forced to select only those she thought had a chance of survival, unable to get the supplies of milk and flavourings she realised would make all the difference. At one point she was attacked by a mob of desperate patients 'clamouring for food in languages I couldn't understand', many of them Poles and Yugoslavs who found it hard to accept that conditions didn't immediately improve now the Germans had gone, and wondered why they couldn't be sent home at once.

Stranded amidst the newly uncovered horror, just behind the front lines, the allied troops had to manage as best they could with a shortage of everything from food to transport and personnel. Janet survived, she says, with the help of a small daily ration of army rum left by her bed each night in a cracked white cup. VE day passed without her noticing, and a field hospital finally moved in. Janet flew back to England in charge of a plane-load of casualties, hoping none of them would need expert attention during the flight.

'The next morning I drove up to London, my hair still full of DDT, to my smart London hairdresser in Sloane Street who took me in without a murmur. I arrived late at a meeting of the Combined Armies at the Royal Society of Medicine, where they were discussing the treatment of starvation. An elderly gentleman was discoursing on the new wonder treatment, hydrolysates – easy to take, easy to give, in every way desirable. I could only get up and shatter his illusions.'

The next day she persuaded the War Office to send dried milk and flavourings as well as hydrolysates to a camp just discovered in Norway, then set off once again to look at more starvation cases in Holland. These were very different from the cases she'd seen in Belsen: 'They at least had had tulip bulbs to eat.' She speaks of the Belsen experience in a matter-of-fact way, though it did, she says, 'give one a sense of priorities in life'.

When she returned home for the last time to take up the post of Principal at her old college, Somerville, she found arguments about the appropriate clothing for female students – whether they should be allowed to wear stockings with or without seams up the back, and so forth – somewhat trivial. She was glad to be reunited with her children and husband, and able to bring her daughters up outside London, where their home had been badly damaged by bombs. 'It is hard,' she says, 'for those who were not alive in 1945 to visualise the desolation of the London scene.

Oxford, undisturbed by war, seemed a dream city in which to build a new life for the family, a dream city in which the children might grow up, a dream city in which I might play my part in University affairs and in scientific work.'

At first, however, she was not entirely happy. David Gourlay had to spend a great deal of his time in London looking after the travel agency, though he came up at weekends to Oxford. To their dismay, they discovered that a college tenant had laid claim to most of the garden belonging to the Principal's house, which somewhat deprived David of his favourite weekend occupation – gardening. And then she discovered that the two laboratories where she had hoped to pursue her own scientific work had no space for her.

The second problem, at least, was solved by two of her Oxford colleagues. Professor Leslie Witts, Nuffield Professor of Clinical Medicine at the Radcliffe Infirmary, asked her to work in his outpatient clinic for blood diseases, so that during her time at Oxford she was able to 'keep her hand in' with actual medical cases. And the Professor of Pharmacology, J. W. Burn, offered her the basement in his Department, where, funded by the Medical Research Council, she proceeded to study the effects of radioactive nuclides on blood and bones, building up a unit for 'Research on the Bone Seeking Radio Nuclides'.

As Principal, she tried to 'open some windows' in Somerville. Soon after her arrival, she hoped to arrange regular meetings with her teaching colleagues to discuss the particular problems of students coming up after the war. 'I suggested Monday, but oh no, "I always go to the Bach choir" and then I tried Tuesday, but that was the night they played bridge, so after that I gave up.'

Nonetheless, she herself tried to be as accessible to her students as possible, often getting up in the middle of the night to listen to their problems and keeping open house. 'People could come in and out and look in the oven, and the only rule I had was that no one should use my bath between six and seven. Very early on I had a dinner party to which I invited several distinguished people from outside Oxford, as well as a Professor from the University, and we had a marvellous time. The next morning, though, my secretary came to me and said: "Principal, did you know that Oxford dinner parties end at ten?" Of course it had got round the whole of Oxford that my party only broke up in the small hours!'

During her time at Somerville, Dame Janet enjoyed the company of some very distinguished academic women, including

Dorothy Hodgkin, who was conducting her pioneering work on vitamin B12, and Enid Starkie, the brilliant modern languages scholar, whose teaching always filled her students with great enthusiams for France and French literature.

Somerville, says Dame Janet Vaughan, seems to breed both a passion for scholarship and a desire to be involved in public affairs. Her 'old girls' include politicians such as Shirley Williams and Margaret Thatcher (an exception, she says, to the fact that most Somervillians tend to be socialists), as well as women like Dr Sheila Cassidy, who was imprisoned and tortured in Chile for treating a wounded guerrilla, and Hannah Stanton, thrown into solitary confinement in South Africa after Sharpeville. 'A father once rang me up because his daughter had been imprisoned in Hungary at the time of the Revolution, and I said: "Oh, of course she will be all right, she is a Somervillian." He told me afterwards this spontaneous reaction on my part had given him great confidence.'

Apart from her role as Principal, she also spent a great deal of time pursuing her research in the laboratory, and writing papers. A college play once portrayed the Principal flying across the stage saying 'just off to the lab!' She was always available on the phone to anyone who needed her back in college, however. She also made herself available, still, to numerous committees, including the University Hebdomadal Council and the Medical Advisory Committee of the University Grants Committee. She became a trustee of the Nuffield Foundation, and fought for the right of foreign students to bring their wives and families to Oxford with them. She was vice-chair, then chairman, of the Regional Hospital Board, and got the first new hospital after the war to be built in Swindon.

'Always have your plans on the drawing board, I've learned. Someone may ring up any moment and offer you money to put them into practice. After the Robbins report, the University Registrar rang me up and asked if we could take in many more women. I said, "Yes, I've got the plans on the drawing board." And so we were able to build new accommodation.'

When she sat on the Royal Commission on Equal Pay just after the war, she felt compelled to table a memorandum of dissent from certain sections of the final report which, in the main, had come down against equal pay. These sections dealt with the explanation of the prevailing differences between the remuneration of men and women, and with the economic and social consequences of equal pay in private industry and commerce. She does not, however, describe herself as a feminist.

'I don't go around agitating about women's rights. I think the best thing women can do is get on with the job in hand. The two women on the Equal Pay Commission who did describe themselves as feminists didn't seem capable of drafting a memorandum of dissent, for all their principles. It was left to me to do – with help from a couple of economists, because I'm not an economist myself.'

When I asked her what she would advise women who find that their ability to get on with their work is hindered by their position as women, she replied that one just had to get round it the best way one could, using one's wits, charm, whatever was available. And she smiled at me – charmingly.

There's no doubt that this is exactly what Dame Janet Vaughan has done. She has never, she says, been ambitious as such. She has seized opportunities, because they interested her at the time. And she has given a great deal in return, in the fields of science, education and social justice, a fact which was recognised as much when Oxford awarded her the Degree of Doctor of Civil Laws Honoris in 1967, as when she was made a Dame of the British Empire ten years earlier.

Since her retirement in 1967 (her husband died four years earlier), she has continued to busy herself with friends and family, receiving an endless flow of postcards from her grandchildren when they travel to other parts of the world and taking an interest in everyone who crosses her path. And she pursues her scientific work with a never-abating enthusiasm. For all her warmth as a human being, she does not like mixing emotion with argument – at least not what she sees as ill-founded emotion. In spite of her knowledge of the dangers of plutonium ('it was always me who handled it in the laboratory, because by then I considered myself too old to worry about developing the cancers') she thinks nuclear power is a boon to humanity. When I asked her about the health risks of radiation, she reminded me that hundreds of coal miners die every year in mining accidents.

'I think we have to take risks in this world,' she said. 'You can't live without risks.'

Which could, I suppose, almost be a motto for her busy life. It occurred to me to ask, as I was leaving, how she had fitted in all these activities, whether risky or not.

'Oh,' she said with a laugh, 'I never played bridge, you see.'

Barbara Wootton

Barbara Wootton, born Barbara Adam in 1897, was educated at the Perse High School and at Girton College, Cambridge. She married Jack Wootton in 1917: he died of wounds the same year. Barbara continued her studies at Girton, at first in classics, later in economics. She worked as a researcher for the Trades Union Congress and Labour Party movement. From 1927 she was associated for many years with London University, first as Director of Studies for Tutorial Classes in the extramural department, later as Reader, then Professor, of Social Studies at Bedford College. She served as a JP over a long period, and has written a number of books on economic, political and social subjects. Her autobiography, *In a World I Never Made*, was published in 1967. She was created a life peer in 1958, taking the title of Baroness Wootton of Abinger, and was made a Companion of Honour in 1977. Baroness Wootton was interviewed for the television series by Ann Clwyd.

> *'I began my career as a voteless adult, precluded by my sex from claiming the University degree to which a uniquely successful academic record would otherwise have entitled me. I became a University professor, the recipient of honorary degrees from Universities on both sides of the Atlantic, and the first woman to sit upon the woolsack. That metamorphosis is the measure of my personal debt to purposive social change.' (1967)*

Barbara Wootton

After twenty minutes in the peers' interview room, Baroness Wootton of Abinger became restless and suggested we go and have tea. This was the first time I had been inside the House of Lords, and I was torn between trying to take in my surroundings, and the need to make the most of the short time Lady Wootton could spend with me before her next engagement. As we walked down the softly-lit corridor towards the dining-room, a jumble of impressions flitted past my distracted senses. The gentle sheen of wood panels, the muted sound of footsteps on thick carpet and low-toned conversations between peer and peer, or (in the member's lobby, for instance) peer and commoner, the latter enlisting the former's support on one issue or another.

It all seemed vaguely unreal. I thought of what Barbara Wootton herself has said about the 'Upper House'. 'No one in his senses,' she wrote in 1967, 'would invent the present House if it did not already exist. But there it is, tremendously seductive in its venerable charm, and oh so civilised!'

She and I certainly had a very civilised tea, sitting opposite a portrait of Henry VII and eating warm, buttery tea-cakes in between snatches of conversation. A gentleman at a nearby table waved to her, and she waved solemnly back before confessing that she couldn't think who he might be. The dining-room was pervaded by the same venerable, mellowed atmosphere as the rest of the House, with the anachronistic exception of a television screen on the wall, from which details of the current debate could be gleaned.

Lady Wootton, like other Labour members amongst the first life peers created in 1958, originally hoped that by accepting her title, she would be doing something to change the nature of the Lords. She felt that as long as this institution retained 'any power or influence', as she put it in an article for *New Society* in 1977, it 'should not remain the almost exclusive preserve of male Tory

Christians'. Yet over tea, she said that, looking back, she probably shouldn't have accepted the title and the role that went with it. She had not enjoyed the role of parliamentarian, and there had been little, in the event, that she could usefully accomplish by sitting on the 'woolsack'.

I wondered if one of the things she had in mind was her bill enabling couples related by marriage (but not by blood) to marry one another, which was thrown out after its second reading in 1981, thanks to opposition from Anglican bishops, among others. 'I've got a good record of losing bills in the House,' she said at the time.

Nonetheless, she still shoulders her responsibilities in what she calls 'the corridors that lead to the corridors that lead to the corridors of power', coming up from her home at Abinger Common in Surrey at least ten days in every month. What was absorbing her the most when I spoke to her, however, was a paper she was writing for a symposium organised by Nottingham University, on the moral basis of the welfare state.

'When they first asked me, I couldn't see the point. Either you agree with the welfare state or you don't. But now I've become quite interested in it. I'm writing some moral philosophy to introduce the subject, which is quite stimulating.'

Her conversation is pretty stimulating too. A stickler for intellectual precision, she picked me up several times during the course of our short time together on the loose use of terms such as 'consumerism'. It was not meant unkindly; she simply wanted to be sure that she understood what we were talking about. Alongside the rigorous mind comes a friendly curiosity un-dimmed by age, and the various annoyances – lapses of memory, physical discomforts – that have accompanied it. Common sense, which she says she has always tried to combine with expertise, is very much in evidence in Barbara Wootton.

'The trouble with you young people,' she said at one point, 'is that you expect me to have eighty-seven years of life spread out in front of me, in such a way that I could remember things at a moment's notice. Well, it's just not like that.'

Her appearance, too, blends practical considerations with a certain warmth and colour. Hers is a serious face, the large, intelligent eyes framed by plain spectacles, the wavy white hair cut neatly, but attractively, short. On the day we met she was wearing a plum velvet suit with a Liberty print blouse. She inspires confidence, without being overbearing.

Not that she always has confidence in herself. Throughout her long life she has given countless lectures and speeches, and in 1967 she was made a Deputy Speaker in the House. Yet in the latter case, she says, the audience rarely gives the impression that you are honestly communicating anything of great importance. As a consequence, she is growing increasingly tired of the sound of her own voice. At least academic audiences actually come to *listen*.

It was as an academic that she began her career. She was born on 14 April 1897, into a highly academic Cambridge family. Her father, Dr James Adam, was senior tutor in classics at Emmanuel College, and her mother, Adela Marion Kensington, also a classics scholar, taught at Girton and later also at Newnham. 'The intense concentration upon academic success,' recalled Barbara Wootton in her autobiography *In a World I Never Made*, 'and particularly upon classical studies which pervaded our childhood, is hard to convey. Even the cat was called Plato.'

Where other children learned nursery rhymes, Barbara and her elder brothers Neil and Arthur learned Greek and Latin irregular verbs. By the time she was ten, she was reading the New Testament in Greek aloud to her father on Sunday evenings. The children were all intellectually precocious, communicating with one another in backwards slang – 'which I understand is commonly used by the criminal classes!' she says, with a laugh. Having two elder brothers was a great boon. 'I learned to flirt in my cradle, playing one off against the other.'

Of her father, who died when she was ten, Barbara Wootton remembers very little, except for a curious routine which took place between him and his children each morning. 'He would come upstairs and ask us what we had done wrong yesterday. So we got into a very good training of having nice little faults prepared for him.' It was her mother's personality that had the major impact on her, however. After her husband's death forced them to leave their house in the grounds of Emmanuel College, Adela Adam bought a house in another part of Cambridge and supported the family with her own teaching.

Whilst the boys were sent away to school (by the time of their father's death, they had already won scholarships to Winchester), Barbara was educated at home, along with a couple of other local girls, by her own mother. 'I was expected to read a great deal for myself, at first chiefly English classics and English history, and later of course Greek and Roman history and literature. I also learned a lot of poetry, including nearly the whole of *Paradise Lost*, by heart. I was docile and industrious, but not always genuinely interested, for much of what I was expected to read or learn was really unsuited to my years. Except for a little amateurish botany, science was totally lacking throughout my education.'

She longed to be sent to boarding school, and offered up (in the privacy of the lavatory) endless prayers to this effect. The prayers were never answered, but when she was thirteen and a half, she was sent to a local day school in Cambridge, which was not much of an educational advance, except for the fact that she caught up in maths, but did at least enable her to mix more freely with girls of her own age. An enduring friend made at this time was Dorothy Russell, later head of the Institute of Pathology at the London Hospital (where Janet Vaughan was, at one point, a colleague).

Barbara describes her mother as 'a great slave driver, intellectually', and although her daughter (as much as her sons) came up to her expectations, the relationship between mother and daughter was not a happy one. Barbara was much closer to her nanny, who was nicknamed 'the Pie' and who was devoted to this, her youngest, charge. She had entered the Adams' employ in her early twenties, and remained there for fifty years or more. The devout Baptist daughter of a Huntingdonshire farm labourer, it was she who supplied both daily discipline and affection.

'She would occasionally become deeply wounded at something you had done, sometimes you didn't even know what. She would be totally withdrawn for two or three days. This used to make me miserable, but I remember, as a sign of becoming mature, one day saying to myself: "This won't last for ever." And of course it never did – it would soon wear out and we'd be on good terms again.'

When the family were hard up, it was Adela's widowed sister Juliet who assisted them. She would finance summer holidays for her siblings and nephews and nieces. It was on one of these, in a rented rectory complete with resident coachman and carriage, that Barbara first remembers becoming conscious of the class distinction.

'We went for a picnic, and the coachman sat a discreet distance away from us, on his own, whilst we ate our picnic. I'm quite sure that he preferred to be on his own, but to my mind that made no difference. I had noticed that there was no contact, and it brought the situation home to me.'

She began to be consumed with a desire to understand the

contemporary world around her, rather than the classical world in which her mother wished her to immerse herself. Her political views began to diverge from those of her conservative parent, who, she remembers, once paced the house 'in anguish at the prospect that the first Old Age Pensions Act would allow old people without other means to receive a pension of as much as five shillings a week.' When the time came for her to think about University entrance, she plucked up the courage to ask if she might not study a subject like History or Economics, rather than Classics. But it was not to be. She was forced to accept the compromise offered by her mother: to read classics for three years, then if she still felt like it, do a year's economics *afterwards*.

Plans had been made for her to go and stay in Germany for a few months after leaving school in the summer of 1914. But the war prevented it, a war which was to plunge her, like many of her famale contemporaries, into the strange limbo of bereavement and loss whose cause she was powerless to prevent or alter in any way. 'My brothers were away, and I had lost the daily companionship of school. I felt as if I belonged nowhere.' In 1915, she nonetheless got her classics scholarship to Girton.

Neil's considerable scientific abilities were employed by work on airships at the Royal Naval Air Service at Kingsnorth in Kent, but Arthur obtained a commission and was sent to the front. So was a close college friend of Neil's, Jack Wootton, to whom Barbara had been introduced whilst he was on leave from the military training which had interrupted his post-graduate History research at Trinity. In 1916, Jack was put out of the war for fourteen months when a shell severed his Achilles tendon. Arthur was not so lucky. In September 1916, he was reported wounded and missing, and was subsequently presumed dead, though his body was never found.

Soon after this, Jack proposed and Barbara accepted him. 'If you were engaged and your parents approved, you could have your fiancé to tea at college, but every time he came, I had to write a little note to the mistress: "Dear Miss Jex-Blake, I should like to have my fiancé Jack Wootton to tea on Tuesday week. May I have your permission?" I always did get permission, but I was given to understand that it should not be asked more than once a fortnight. Later, I thought this attitude most callous, given the circumstances of the war.'

In the late summer of 1917, Jack was deemed fit for active service once more, and he received orders to rejoin his regiment in France towards the end of September. Barbara's mother then suggested that perhaps they ought to marry sooner rather than later, since if he were to be wounded, she would, as his wife, be allowed to go to him. Barbara was nonetheless to carry on with her studies afterwards.

In the event, only two days after their marriage on 5 September 1917, Barbara Wootton put her young husband on the train at Victoria along with 'the rest of the cannon-fodder'. A telegram had arrived the day before the wedding, curtailing even the two weeks' honeymoon they had originally planned. It was the last time she ever saw him.

'Five weeks later the War Office "regretted to inform me" that Capt. J. W. Wootton of the 11th Battalion Suffolk Regiment had died of wounds. He had been shot through the eye and died forty-eight hours later on an ambulance train; and in due course his blood-stained kit was punctiliously returned to me.'

In the space of ten years, she had, 'learned little about life, much about death'. Not surprisingly, the experience left a deep scar: 'It left me with a total mistrust of life, a certainty that something will go wrong, something awful will happen.'

She still had to sit her classics finals, though now she gave up being resident at Girton. Just before the exams, she developed tonsillitis, and in some sense avenged herself for the academic pressure her mother had put on her. 'I had taken the first part of the exam, when the doctor came to see me to ask if I wanted to continue. "Medically I ought to say you shouldn't take it," he said, "but if it means a great deal to you, I don't really think in the long run it would do you any harm." And knowing the grief it would cause my mother if I didn't complete the exam, I said, very stiffly: "No, you must do what is medically right." I think it's the only deliberately malicious thing I've ever done.' So she received an *aegrotat* (the pass given to those too ill to sit all the papers) rather than the coveted Classics First she had been expected to obtain.

She was now free to pursue her interest in economics. Armistice Day was not the only time she felt jubilation in 1918. 'I remember the enormous sense of relief when I shut my classical dictionary with a bang and picked up G. D. H. Coles's *World of Labour*, took it out to a deck-chair in the garden and began to read. Now I felt free.' At the end of the year, she not only got a First, but was also awarded a special mark of distinction that no one before her had ever received. She still wasn't a BA, however, since at that time women, though permitted to study in their own colleges and take the exams, were not awarded degrees by the University.

After a brief period on a research scholarship at the London School of Economics, combined with some lecturing at Westfield College in the University of London, she was still wondering what direction to take in life. Her socialist convictions were growing, but she didn't know how to apply them. 'I was still lamentably ignorant of any of the practical aspects of economics, and my first-hand acquaintance with severe poverty or slum life was virtually non-existent.'

Girton, however, invited her back to take the post of Director of Studies in Economics, and since she couldn't think what else to do, she accepted. The life that ensued was extremely comfortable, with a good salary, pleasant rooms, and always plenty of hot water on hand. 'As I lay and soaked each night, I read myself a lecture on the dangers of being seduced by this sybaritic indulgence.'

Being short-staffed, with many students just returned from the war, the University Economics Board took the unprecedented step of asking Barbara Wootton, to whom the University itself, by virtue of her sex, was not prepared to grant the title of BA, let alone anything else, to give a course of lectures. This resulted in a strange situation whereby a male economist, in order to satisfy the outrage of the General Board of Studies, had to put *his* name down as lecturer, with a footnote to the effect that the lectures would in fact be given by Mrs Wootton. The money she earned from these lectures enabled her to buy her own typewriter. She was, however, getting restless in this cushioned existence, and even activities in the University Labour Club didn't entirely satisfy her craving for wider horizons.

'I was brimming over with socialist fervour, for which the life of a Cambridge don did not then seem to offer many outlets. More and more I began to creep away to London, whenever I could be free, taking extramural classes, getting myself mixed up with the Workers' Educational Association and similar bodies, and returning on the last train to Cambridge dead tired, but far more satisfied than after a day's work in college.'

She applied for the post of research worker in what was then the joint research department of the Trades Union Congress and the Labour Party. At her interview she was asked why she had applied, and she said that 'a multitude of converging considerations' had prompted her. Afterwards Hugh Dalton, for whom she had worked when he stood in a Cambridge by-election, and who was on the selection committee, took her aside and told her she should have named 'the unbearable injustices of our social system' as her motive, which would in any case have been equally true, she says. In spite of what she has described as 'my apparently cold-blooded and pompous intellectualism', she did get the job.

The job was not nearly as well paid as her previous one, but she found some modest lodgings and set to work, under the benign supervision of Arthur Greenwood. The first memorandum she produced (a critique of the 'Social Credit' theories of Major Douglas) was sent back to her by Sidney Webb, who had found it unsatisfactory. 'Why I was not more downcast by this episode right at the beginning of my career at Eccleston Square is hard to explain: I can only suppose that I was so enchanted to find myself actually working for the Labour Movement that nothing could damp my enthusiasm.'

During this period, from 1922 to 1926, she was, as she puts it, 'incurably serious-minded and still suffering I think from delayed emotional shock from Jack's death'. She had plenty of opportunity to observe, at close quarters, the effects of parliamentary aspirations during general elections.

'I would go out in the evenings to the candidates' meetings, taking the notes I had written for the speakers with me, and listen to see what they did with them. I realised this kind of thing was not for me – I couldn't have brought myself to use such absolutely false answers to the questions that were asked. I know it's a part of the trade, but it cured me forever of any desire to stand myself.'

In 1924, she bought her first car, an air-cooled, two-cylinder Rover (the cheapest and smallest car she could find), and was also asked to sit on her first major committee, the Departmental Committee on the National Debt and Taxation. As the only woman – and somewhat younger and less well-known than the other members of the committee – she came in for some unsavoury press attention, with headlines such as: 'Secrets of Debt Enquiry Woman: Does she ever play?'

By 1927, the committee had failed to reach agreement, and the four Labour members signed a minority report which she had drafted, drawing attention to the burden of taxation borne by those with small incomes. This, however, was the last minority report she was ever to sign.

Early in 1926, her local Labour Party put her name forward to be a Justice of the Peace, and the nomination was accepted by the Lord Chancellor. As with her lectures in Cambridge six years earlier, the anomalies of attitudes towards women were in evidence, since although women had had the vote since 1918, it was only granted to women of thirty or over. Exclusion of the women characterised as 'flappers' was, she says, an example of 'British reluctance to do anything properly in the first place', since she herself was only twenty-eight when she was made a JP. 'At an age when I was not considered old enough or wise enough to cast a Parliamentary vote, I was nevertheless deemed fit to sit in judgement on my fellows.'

This was also the year of the General Strike. She had worked on the miners' campaign leading up to this under the slogan 'Not a penny off the pay, not a minute on the day', but once the strike was under way she and the other members of the office were mostly occupied running messages to and from local strike head-quarters in and around London. She carried both a TUC pass to safeguard her from any accusation of blacklegging, and a JP's badge which gave her 'authority to quell any disturbances' she might encounter. 'This set me wondering how I should decide, if I ran into a threatening crowd, which of these two documents would be likely to be the more efficacious!'

By now, however, she was getting restless again. She liked working for Arthur Greenwood, in spite of his habit of springing work on her at the end of the day, when he could quite well have given it to her earlier. But there was little prospect for advance-ment in her department, and the challenge and attraction of writing material that other people would deliver or sign their names to was wearing thin.

She applied for, and was offered, the job of Principal at Morley College for Working Men and Women. In a sense, the position was the culmination of a growing interest in adult education. Over the last few years, as well as lecturing at places like Bedford College (where her mother had lectured before her), she had taught many extramural classes in the London area and continued to be active in the Workers' Educational Association.

The purpose of the college was to provide educational oppor-tunities for those whose education had previously been curtailed or restricted. Students attended on a part-time basis in the evenings (and on Saturdays there were sports and social events). All the staff, apart from the Principal and her secretary, were also employed part-time. Barbara Wootton made a clean sweep, attempting to straighten out the records and the accounts, which had got into a state of considerable confusion under the previous incumbent. She also dismissed those members of staff she felt had got stale, a move she now sees as somewhat ruthless. 'I have come to be more concerned about the world's incompetents and the question whether every employer must not expect to carry his proportion of them.'

She also had to deal with the slight tension between the two functions of the college – educational and social. The LCC (as London's local authority was then called) stipulated that the former must remain the principal purpose of the college. But many working people found at the college the only form of social life they could afford. Even Barbara Wootton's own classes were at one point attended by a young mother who told her that since she could no longer afford to go to the cinema, this was the cheapest way she could find of spending the one evening when she could get a baby-sitter.

There was also the problem of the split between the college orchestra, whose reputation under conductors of the standing of Gustav Holst had ensured an atmosphere of exclusivity often generated by dedication, and the rest of the students. They tended to resent the musicians' habit of dropping the reference to 'working men and women' in the title of the college.

In 1927, she was invited by the Council of the League of Nations to attend a World Economic Conference, the first of its kind, in Geneva. The other two women invited were Dutch and Austrian, and they were immediately adopted by their respective governments into their official delegations. Not so Barbara Wootton. The British government left her to pay all her own expenses, which she just managed to do with the help of the Women's International League. They did, however, acknowledge her existence rather belatedly and issued her with a cheque once the conference had ended.

She was now offered a marvellous job as Director of Studies for Tutorial Classes in the extramural department of the University of London. It was a golden opportunity, fairly well paid, but more importantly with no condition attached (as there was at Morley) that a woman in the post must resign on marriage. On the other hand, she found it somewhat embarrassing to leave Morley, where she was grappling with challenging, but enjoyable issues after less than two years. 'The fact, too, that I had so completely turned the place upside down during my short tenure of office seemed only to aggravate the iniquity of leaving someone else to face the consequences.'

In the new job, where she was to remain for the next seventeen years, she had responsibility for overseeing the academic content of at least thirty (and later twice that number) classes spread all over London, which meant a great deal of travelling, usually in the evenings. 'Perhaps the strongest impression that these years have left,' she later wrote, 'is one of waiting in cold, dark and rain at eleven o'clock at night on deserted and ill-lit suburban railway stations for trains that did not come.'

Lady Wootton regards adult education as a valuable experience for any teacher of Higher Education – a corrective to academic complacency, perhaps. 'If your extramural lectures are boring or do not give the students what they want, the class vanishes and so does your fee. The extramural teacher has, therefore, a strong inducement to pay attention to his quality as a teacher as well as to his competence in his subject.'

In 1933, she published her first book – a collection of short stories called *Twos and Threes*. It wasn't particularly successful, but from this point on she continued to write, though fiction took second place to books on economics and social science. Meanwhile she had begun to travel extensively, first to an adult education conference in Chicago in 1930, and then to the Soviet Union in 1932, again with a group of educationalists. They travelled third class from Ostend to Leningrad.

'Travel facilities were very hard. We sometimes had to make journeys of up to twelve hours with no refreshments other than the occasional cup of tea. I remember I was very popular in the train, because I had taken a large supply of almonds and raisins which is very nourishing when you can't get anything else.

'There wasn't much that I liked about the Soviet Union at that stage. At schools we visited, the children would ask us if we came from England where they beat the children? And I couldn't say no. You felt like replying that at least we didn't station a child with a bayonet outside the door of a children's home, which is one of the things we saw.

'They were obviously making a lot of their industry, but I wanted to see living conditions, not machinery. We said we would very much like to see a collective farm, which was one of the big changes they were making. At first they said the roads were snowbound, but when we said there was nothing else we wanted to see, so we might as well leave the country, they relented. Incidentally, the snow never showed up at all!'

She could see nothing amiss in the collective farm, and though she didn't think that this was her idea of 'what they're pleased to call socialism', she felt that 'what might appear to be guilty attempts at concealment are often merely the result of simple laziness.'

When she got home, she started work on her book *Plan or No Plan*, published in 1934, which compared the economic system of post-revolutionary Russia with the one at home. 'These, it should be remembered, were the days of the economic crises and depressions of the 1930s, days in which Governments sought to remedy desperate unemployment by the lunatic expedient of reducing everybody's income and spending, private or public. Wars apart, in all my life public policy has never – until today – been more abysmally stupid. Small wonder that many eyes were turned hopefully towards the Russian experiment.'

Plan or No Plan, in which she predicted that it would be the United States which would pull most effectively out of economic depression, and expressed scepticism about some of the Soviet ideals such as the 'withering away' of the State, was 'essentially the work of a democratic socialist, of a liberal mind with a small "l"; and in the bottom of my heart I had my doubts as to whether sweet reasonableness would prevail against the forces of evil.'

So she answered herself with a novel, *London's Burning*, which, at a time when Mosley's blackshirts were very much in evidence, dealt with the effect of a Fascist uprising on a group of liberal-minded people.

During some of the evening classes in the extramural department, she had met an attractive young student named George Wright. During the department's summer school in 1934, she got to know him better, and when the school was over, they went on holiday together in Norfolk, and decided to get married. George, who had been awarded a scholarship at the London School of Economics, was at this point driving a taxi for his living. The press got a lot of mileage out of this, hounding the 'cabby' and the 'don' to the point where the former had to climb into his own house by the back wall in order to try and avoid them. Later on in his career, George became a Councillor and then an Alderman of the LCC, but the unconventional marriage which had broken class barriers continued to make good copy. 'Twenty-three years after our marriage, when I was one of the first women admitted to the House of Lords, and George had not been near a taxi except as a passenger for nearly twenty years, I was pestered with requests for us both to be photographed outside the House, standing "beside his taxi".'

They did, however, manage to keep the date of their marriage a secret, and in July 1935 the knot was tied in Fulham registry office by the only woman registrar in the country, followed by lunch in the LCC catering school. Meanwhile Barbara's mother is said to have lunched in the market-place in Cambridge to show she was not perturbed at all the adverse publicity her daughter was getting.

During the next couple of years, George and Barbara travelled a great deal together, and Barbara continued to write, producing her *Lament for Economics* in 1938, in which she said that 'the study of economics should not be undertaken in a spirit of indifference to its practical utility as a means of improving the conditions of life'. Economic conditions could only be explained with the help of rigorous research into social, political and psychological factors. She wanted to establish an economic methodology (which would also be a sound basis for a planned economy) that avoided what she felt were groundless assumptions made by economists such as Lionel Robbins in his *Nature and Significance of Economic Science*. 'In what purported to be purely objective accounts of the working of a free enterprise economy,' she has said, 'one could too often detect the hand of the apologist.'

After this book, she turned her attention from economics proper to social science in general. Her thinking in this area was enhanced by her numerous experiences of public service. In 1938 she sat on the Royal Commission on Workmen's Compensation, and after the war she was a member of a National Assistance Appeal Tribunal and acted as an employed person's representative under the Unemployment Insurance Acts. She also became a magistrate in the London Juvenile Courts, an experience which led her to form strong views on the rehabilitation of young offenders.

On one of her trips to the USA during the 1930s, she and George used the money she had earned lecturing to make a trip to Mexico, travelling from Vera Cruz to Mexico City on a train which kept breaking down. 'On one of these unscheduled halts a happy hour was spent watching an Indian woman repairing her hut with fresh banana leaves carefully trimmed and disposed. I do not know why she made so deep an impression, but even now thirty years afterwards, the image of that woman sometimes comes to mind as I perform my own household chores, and I have the feeling that we should have understood one another; for feminine tasks are much the same the world over, and at every level those upon whom they devolve have much in common.'

On her way back from this trip, she and George went to be cleared by US tax officials. George was asked if he had earned anything, and replied truthfully that he hadn't. They never thought to ask 'the little woman' if *she* had earned anything, so she left the country without paying any tax and on her return invested the fruits of the American official's misogyny in their first refrigerator. 'I told this story on American television some years later, but they never did anything about it!'

During the Second World War, both she and George were conscientious objectors, but she discovered that she was exempted as a magistrate in any case. The war years were something of a hiatus for her. She abandoned a book she had been trying to write on politics, and her job became fairly meaningless since conditions were not suited to evening classes in London. She did, however, work for a while at Chatham House (the Royal Institute of International Affairs) as secretary to 'Study Groups on Reconstruction'. But her main interest during the war was in the Federal Union, which tried to work towards a federation of states, and ultimately world government. This was the only direction, she felt, that would lead the world away from perpetual wars.

'Some of us thought we could reach our goal one way, e.g. via an Anglo-American or English-speaking federation, while others looked more hopefully to the establishment of a European Federation. But to the hard-headed practical men we were all alike; a hopeless lot of woolly idealists, if not actually near-traitors. Of course the practical men were right; they always are, if only because they can make themselves so. Practical men in positions of power can always demonstrate the impracticability of idealistic proposals by the simple device of making sure these are never tried.'

Yet in the light of today's EEC, whatever its actual drawbacks, the proposals of the Federal Union do not seem so way out. As Barbara Wootton points out, 'it is the foolish dreams of one generation which become the commonplaces of the next'. Meanwhile she continued to back the 'foolish dreams' of her generation with hard-headed research and critical thinking, for instance in her attack on prevailing wage theories, *The Social Foundations of Wage Policy*, published in 1955. In her reflection on why people are paid what they are paid, she noted that as a university lecturer, she earned the same amount as the elephant which gave rides to children at Whipsnade Zoo.

In 1944 she returned to fully-fledged academic work and obtained a Readership at Bedford College, a post which four years later was upgraded to the rank of Professor. The work entailed overseeing the training of prospective social workers, and although she had had some contact with this area in her capacity as a magistrate, much of it was new to her.

'Some of the attitudes that prevailed in the world of professional social work I found decidedly disquieting, and difficult to reconcile with the socialist equalitarianism which was the basis of my social philosophy.' She disliked, for instance, the term 'case' and 'case-load' in connection with the receipt of assistance from a social worker. This was one of the attitudes she was to criticise in her best-known work, *Social Science and Social Pathology*, published in 1959.

Before that, however, she had written *Testament for Social Science*, in which she developed the view that the social sciences needed as many resources as the natural sciences, if they were to do their job properly and give empirically accurate pictures of social conditions in an increasingly complex civilisation. Yet she encountered a great deal of hostility from other University departments when she and her colleagues in the Sociology Department tried to set up a small field research unit with the help of government funds earmarked for the expansion of the social sciences. Thus in 1952, she gladly turned her back on administrative struggles and their political undercurrents, and availed herself of a Nuffield Foundation grant which funded the research she needed to do for *Social Science and Social Pathology*. During the next five years she made a thorough study of the relatively young social sciences. This led to a detailed assessment of the direction they were taking. One of her conclusions was that people were more in need of material help than complicated advice on how to manage their lives better.

Throughout the late forties and fifties she continued to combine committee work with her academic research. From 1946–9 she sat on the Interdepartmental Committee on Shop Hours; the 1947 Royal Commission on the Press was followed in 1954 by the Royal Commission on the Civil Service. Her interest in broadcasting – she often appeared on the *Brains Trust* – culminated with a period as a Governor of the BBC from 1950–6.

In her public capacity, she continued to travel all over the world. In 1947, she took part in a training course for West Indian social workers in Jamaica, though she was unsure whether detailed knowledge of English social institutions was something from which the students could really benefit. She also lectured in the USA, once undertaking a long tour in which she found herself reduced to the level of a 'speaking parcel'. Here again, though for slightly different reasons, she had her doubts as to whether what she was saying was really worth hearing.

In 1956, she was invited with a small delegation to India, where the government wanted to familiarise the British with their current situation and future plans. In Bangalore, she got to know a woman engaged in family planning propaganda in the neighbouring villages. 'It had not previously occurred to me that methods of contraception might be used as a form of social introduction but, as my guide presented her various friends and acquaintances amongst the village women to me, she would say "This is Mrs So-and-So, who uses the rhythm method".'

Once again in an academic capacity, in 1958 she travelled to Ghana, where although she loved the rain forest and the village life she managed to glimpse between work engagements, she was disappointed by the attitudes of her students, who were more interested in passing exams than in discussing the future of their country. The same disappointment extended itself to their leader, Prime Minister Nkrumah, whose subsequent record she describes as 'a melancholy cautionary tale about what may be the end of a road to which vanity is the gateway.'

She had now reached the age of sixty. She decided to resign her University post but she still had another five years to go as Chairman of a Juvenile Court in London. She was looking forward to retirement in slow stages. Then Hugh Gaitskell summoned her to the House of Commons to tell her that he was including her name amongst those proposed by the Opposition to be admitted to the House of Lords under the recently passed Life Peerages Act. She was one of four women on the list. No sooner had she resigned one duty than she found herself with a whole new role in life. It was not possible for Barbara Wootton to be idle.

'On the first occasion that Her Majesty opened Parliament after the admission of women,' wrote Baroness Wootton nearly a decade later, 'we waited with considerable curiosity to see whether she would vary the traditional formula. She did not. "My Lords, pray be seated," she said, as usual.'

She herself and her female colleagues have firmly rejected the use of the title of 'peeress' since this is the title normally given to the wives of male peers, who should be distinguished, they feel, from women who have achieved a title in their own right. 'George used to joke that he was "the world's first male peeress", and he was quite right! On the rare occasions when it is necessary to identify sex, I much prefer the title woman peer.'

Towards the end of the fifties, she bought an old barn at Abinger Common in Surrey, to which she had planned to retire after she had converted and renovated it. When she finally moved there, however, it was without George. They had lived together happily enough for twenty-one years, and yet what had been incipient strains on the marriage now became such that they decided they no longer wanted to live together, though they never divorced and remained on good terms until his death in 1964 from cancer. 'On my side, I am too much occupied with my own affairs and too reluctant to modify my way of life, to make an easy marriage partner. George on the other hand was clearly a natural polygamist. From the earliest days of our marriage he had always found it necessary to have what I can only call a secondary wife around the corner . . . In a world in which inevitably more limelight fell upon me than upon him, their function was not difficult to understand.'

Perhaps one of the reasons for this limelight is the fact that she has so frequently been a 'first' or an 'only'. In 1963 she was the first lay person (not to mention the first woman) to give the Hamlyn Trust lectures, taking as her subject *Crime and the Criminal Law* and drawing on her long experience both as a magistrate and as a social scientist. However, she feels that the things she does are often misinterpreted and sensationalised, as in the case of the Wootton Committee, which didn't, she reminded me, propose the legalisation of cannabis, only the relaxation of penalities for its possession. What fellow social scientist Peter Townsend has called her 'steely independence of mind' has led her to be as critical of fashionable liberal assumptions as of old-fashioned conservative ones.

She has remained as active in her new capacity as she ever was in her previous roles. Throughout the sixties and seventies, she continued to travel extensively, always sampling, wherever possible, the juvenile courts and prisons of the countries she visited, be they Australia or Japan (both trips she made in 1961), China or Ethiopia (which she visited during the seventies). Wherever she goes, she takes a keen interest in the local culture, appraising the system and comparing it with others she has seen in other parts of the world. China, especially, 'made me very hopeful, I felt they were on the right track, though I'm told they've slipped back somewhat now.'

Her position in the House of Lords has also led her to be deluged with requests for help from individuals who feel that she might be able to use her influence and considerable abilities to improve legislation affecting them – as in the case of the widower who wished to marry his stepdaughter. Her failure on this score is by no means untypical of what happens to reforming spirits in the Lords (or in British Parliament in general, come to that). Nonetheless, although the general Bill had failed, she succeeded later with a personal Bill legitimising this one marriage. It is with causes like these that she continues to participate in a public life which, in her mid-eighties, she finds somewhat stressful. 'Yet if I were to leave the Lords, what should I do? I could only die.'

In a world where politics is said to be the art of the possible, one can understand why Baroness Barbara Wootton never stood for parliament, and only entered the political arena as a matter of public service and on the side-lines, so to speak. She has never been content with other people's definitions of what is 'possible'. When I spoke to her, however, she didn't have a very optimistic view of her place in the history books. 'Honestly, when I ask myself what has BW been able to effect, really, in this life of hers, it amounts to about that much –' and she pressed finger and thumb together over her tea-cup. And in this nuclear age of ours, she often despairs of her fellow men. 'Tell me,' she said, 'have you any idea how one resigns from the human race?'

Personally, I'd prefer to leave her in the less pessimistic vein that was in evidence at the end of her autobiography, where she said that in half a century of public and professional life, she had not found the 'art of the possible' to be as restricted as some would imagine.

'The limits of the possible constantly shift, and those who ignore them are apt to win in the end. Again and again I have had the satisfaction of seeing the laughable idealism of one generation evolve into the accepted commonplace of the next. But it is from the champions of the impossible rather than from the slaves of the possible that that evolution draws its creative force.'

May that judgement stand for herself, as much as for all her contemporaries portrayed in this book. And for the sake of those who inherit this tradition of laughable idealism, and who are inspired by such rich and varied contributions to this eventful century of ours, let us hope this judgement is correct.